BETWEEN

Getting From Where You Are To Where You Want To Be

Denise Lewis Christopher

authorHOUSE

AuthorHouse™
1663 Liberty Drive
Bloomington, IN 47403
www.authorhouse.com
Phone: 1-800-839-8640

© 2009 Denise Lewis Christopher. All rights reserved.

No part of this book may be reproduced, stored in a retrieval system, or transmitted by any means without the written permission of the author.

First published by AuthorHouse 7/21/2009

ISBN: 978-1-4389-7945-8 (sc)
ISBN: 978-1-4389-7946-5 (hc)

Printed in the United States of America
Bloomington, Indiana

This book is printed on acid-free paper.

Unless otherwise indicated, all Scripture quotations are taken from the HOLY BIBLE, NEW LIVING TRANSLATION VERSION (NLT)

Bible verses noted KJV are taken from the King James Version.

Bible verses noted NIV are taken from the New International Version.

Italics used in scripture verses reflect author's emphasis only.

Author's Photograph taken by Kenya D. Anderson

Book Cover Designed and Illustrated by Denise Lewis Christopher

Especially For You, Mama

(I miss you so much. And I'm still trying to become the great woman that you were. I can only hope that I've made you proud.)

For Tang,
Because You Believed That I Could Do This

Dedication

This book is devoted to the loving memory of my dear parents, Charles and Rose Lewis; and to the memory of my two sisters, Beverly Lewis Green and Rosemarie Lewis Wilson. Only God knows how much I miss all of you.

I also dedicate this project to my other siblings; Nathan, Theron, Raphael, Carolyn, Wayne, John, Ronald, Arnold, and Kelson (the last button on Jacob's coat, as our mother used to call him). I love you all. All of you are a huge part of the many fond memories I have of growing up in the house on Lizardi Street. Those same memories have given me something to laugh about whenever I needed a boost. Thank you!

Acknowledgements

First, I acknowledge God, who is the greatest lover of my soul. He has directed my every step in bringing this project to completion. I am grateful to Him for allowing every trial, mistake, disappointment and setback in my life, because all of these have given me something to give back to you, the reader.

Second, I thank my children, who contributed greatly to this project. My daughter, Kenya, is a really good writer, and I can't tell you how many times I interrupted her homework, her Michael Buble' music, and her beloved "Degrassi" episodes, to ask her to read portions of my manuscript as it came to life. She is my resident editor! My son, Kevin Joshua, kept me energized throughout this entire venture, contributing his ideas and his contagious zeal! His easy wit and belief in me helped me to stay the course. Kenya and Josh, you two have taught me some of my greatest life lessons. You are the best children any mother could ever have.

Additional gratitude to some very special people:

O'Donovan M. Christopher, my wonderful husband, - for supporting my vision to use my gifts to fulfill my life's purpose. I love you!

Kwame Aygeman, John Cannady, Jr., Rose L. Wilson, and Carolyn L. Jasmin - for reviewing the roughest draft of my manuscript. Your input was so encouraging to me!

Ms. Angela Moore - your insights into a subsequent draft was most valuable to me! I owe you big time!

Mr. Robert Ewan, my friend and colleague - I cannot tell you how many times I went to him with my computer related questions. And he was always willing to help out. (Okay, so I'm a little technically challenged!). Thanks, Rob!

Ms. Catherine Hensley (my very capable editor) – For the meticulous care you gave to my manuscript! Much appreciation to you, my dear.

Mrs. Althea Haywood, (New Israel Baptist Church, New Orleans, La.) - for pulling me out of the corner to resume teaching God's word. (You had no idea that at the time all I wanted to do was to find the smallest hole for me and my children, and make the rest of the world go away!) Thank you.

Pastor Frank A. Davis, III, (Bibleway Missionary Baptist Church, New Orleans, La.) - for encouraging me 30 years ago, to do whatever the Lord tells me to do. I would have never imagined that that one admonition would have led me to this place in His Honorable Service.

Mr. Shawn Hollingsworth, Mrs. Patricia Scott, Mr. Andrew Walker, and Mrs. Cynthia Walker – Just when I'd nearly run out of energy, heaven dispatched these four angels to help me to review the final galley proof of this project. Much love to each of you!

To all of you, my readers – you didn't know this, but you kept me pushing through this project, even when I wanted to quit!

Contents

INTRODUCTION	xv
1. Unsuspecting Realities	1
2. Pressed Between	5
3. Broken	15
4. You Don't Have to Fear the Stuff in the Middle	20
5. Mistakes, Messes and Miracles	25
6. Shame, Shame, Shame	30
7. A Window of Time and a Door of Opportunity	40
8. Keepers	49
9. The Appearance of Things	54
10. Do You Know What You Really Want To Do?	62
11. Moving Forward	69
12. My Story, Your Story	74
13. Biblical Characters Who Were Between Some Things	84
14. Habakkuk's Hardships	87
15. David's Dilemma	92
16. Joseph's Jolts	99
17. Hannah's Hell	107
18. Ruth's Redemption	114
19. My Reflections on the Biblical Characters	120
20. Afterthoughts	125
ADDENDUM	
❖ A Very Special Dedication	129

Introduction

(Suggestions on how to best use this book)

I'm making the assumption that if you're reading this book you might be on a kind of personal quest to gain more fulfillment, joy, or contentment in your life. Or, perhaps you've picked it up out of mere curiosity. My assumption may be wrong, but whatever the reason, allow me to make a few suggestions on how this book might best serve you, because if you're feeling stuck *between* some things, then you will definitely want to keep reading.

First, I encourage you to read it with only you in mind. Initially, don't think about how it might be a good read for someone else you know. I've written it especially for *you*.

Next, I've noted tiny portions of the text for emphasis. Some quotes are my own; but you'll notice that some are credited to others. Make immediate note of whatever thoughts that might impress you by underlining, highlighting, or writing them in the book margins or on a separate sheet of paper. You can revisit them later. Trust that certain thoughts grab you for a reason and that this may have to do with the season you're in right now.

In addition, I'm hoping that as you're reading, thoughts and questions will naturally pop up in your mind, but I've tried to assist you at the end of most of the chapters by sharing some questions and thoughts for your consideration. You will notice that I've included some challenges or "dares", which I encourage you to consider doing. It is in doing that we learn best; it gives "stickability" (*my made up word*), or

xv

staying power to the life lessons we can pick up along our journeys. And it can aid us in the healing process as well.

Finally, I've tried to write so that each chapter could stand on its own legs; independent of one another. Therefore, you don't have to read it straight through as you would a novel; that is, unless you want to. My hope is that you will be inspired to keep this book as a resource guide to circle back to from time to time, because some points that may not speak to you at this particular juncture in your life may prove to be very useful to you later on. It's an easy read, so just imagine that a trusted friend is sharing these thoughts with you.

With that said, let me also say that my hope is that by the end of our encounter here, you will choose to add me to your list of trusted friends.

Denise

Chapter One

Unsuspecting Realities

> *If I were to take a poll of all races, socio-economic statuses, and educational levels, most of us would be surprised by how many would anonymously admit they are hurting; and hurting deeply.*

My forty eight years have placed me in the company of enough people to know that, in general, many are hurting. However, we can't always tell by looking at them that they are. If I were to take a poll of all races, socio-economic statuses, and educational levels, most of us would be surprised by how many would anonymously admit they are hurting; and hurting deeply. There are just too many things to hide behind. But I believe that many people would come out of hiding if they could see how valuable they really are, and know that it's okay when life veers off the course which they previously envisioned for themselves.

In this book, I write about everyday experiences. Whether loss, insecurity, fear, depression, loneliness, or frustration over mistakes made, it's likely that you, a colleague at work, a neighbor, or someone you've passed in the corridors of life, is hurting right now. Let's face it, life happens. It happens with its plethora of joys and accomplishments, but it also comes with its share of disappointments, setbacks and tragedies.

1

Between: Getting From Where You Are To Where You Want To Be

I call these experiences our *unsuspecting realities*. They are reminders to some of us, and revelations to others, that obstacles are a natural part of the journey to success and fulfillment. We should learn to embrace them!

Life doesn't make appointments with us, nor does it seek permission to throw us a curve ball at 98 miles per hour. Life doesn't care if you're a chief executive officer, the president or prime minister of a great nation, a struggling college student, a stay-at-home mom, a clergyman, a business owner, or a janitor. It creates situations that force all of us to reevaluate our life choices and perspectives. Often though, if allowed, this propels us toward our life's purpose.

I've also been around long enough to know that many people aren't satisfied with their lives, in general, right now. Most can't quite put their hands on it, but somewhere along their merry way they discovered, even if only subconsciously, that there is a disconnect somewhere. But where? Is it in one of their relationships? In their career? Can it be frustration with their current status in life?

What about you? Has your security been in your bank account? Is it in having the privilege of living in a gated community? Or, is it in your mate? You believe you should be happy at this stage in your life, but for some reason, you're not.

The answers you will discover might surprise you. I can't tell you where your disconnection is, but I *can* tell you that with sheer determination, brutal honesty and regular, divine "quiet time," you will discover it. Then you will find yourself embarking on a journey to living your life with a renewed and redefined purpose. Etching out your own daily "quiet time" isn't some sort of penance but rather a useful tool to help free you whenever you feel trapped between the different phases of your life.

Life doesn't make appointments with us, nor does it seek permission to throw us a curve ball at 98 miles per hour. It creates situations that force all of us to reevaluate our life choices and perspectives. Often, though, this propels us toward our life's purpose.

2

I believe that God uses each person's life to speak to them, but we each need to be quiet long enough, and often enough, to hear what it's saying. Life often *screams* messages at us, but we can become so out of tune with ourselves, and so bombarded with even louder noises from both within, and outside of ourselves, that we simply cannot hear the messages. How then can we heed a message, if we can't hear it?

You may need to spend more quality time with *you;* nobody but you alone. Get to know yourself better than any other human being knows you. Are you always on the lookout to find someone to spend time with you? Sure, you may very well be alone physically, when you'd rather not be, but are you getting the spiritual benefit from it? Are you taking advantage of that precious alone time? Or, are you preoccupied with complaining about it and thinking that you would be more valuable if you had a companion in your life? Allow God to become that perfect soul mate for you. Create a space for yourself that you can retreat to daily to draw from God's power at work in you. You need to hear those life messages that are custom-made just for you.

My goal in this book is two-fold. First, it's my desire to convince you that you are extremely valuable and that your life is still very useful. And that you are okay, though you may not be *feeling* okay about your life as it is right now. I'm aware, that when you're in the midst of experiencing any loss or disappointment that life throws your way, it's very easy to want to give up. However, painful transitions are an inevitable part of the life experience. Despite them, you can still come out experiencing peace, recovery and success in the end. And if you think you've reached your plateau in life, think again.

Secondly, I believe that life and loss give us a window of time to heal, and then inevitably, doors of opportunities are opened for us, allowing us to make great contributions to the world. I also believe that people who are hurting best serve themselves by helping other hurting people. This ultimately moves them toward their best healing. It is my hope that you will seize this chance to impact the world positively, using the most challenging parts of your journey to lay the foundation for your best contributions.

I titled this book "*Between*" because in life we are guaranteed to experience interludes; whether spiritual, physical, emotional, financial,

Between: Getting From Where You Are To Where You Want To Be

or professional. Sometimes life can make us feel like we're literally squeezed between some things, like a set of hardbound books pressed tightly between two huge and heavy bookends! And often we feel stuck right there in the middle; between where we are and the place we'd like to be. I can't help but think that so many people are bewildered and heavy laden because, in general, they're not equipped to handle those *between* phases of their lives. Perhaps they fail to see their specific interludes as divinely inspired and appointed moments hiding behind difficult situations.

We need to move through life with purposeful caution as we ponder our next move following loss or setbacks. Whenever we're pressed between life's challenges, we have the freedom to make either positive or negative choices. Therefore, how we choose to handle our transitions is crucial to our well-being and to the healing process.

It is my prayer that some of the lessons I've learned will be of inspiration to you. I write about everyday situations, the kind of things most of us can relate to. My hope is that you'll find your story embedded in mine.

Chapter Two

Pressed Between

> *Living pressed between some uncomfortable things allows us time to think and perhaps redefine the areas of our lives that we previously thought we had a handle on.*

What do you do when you are living between doubt and faith, affirmation and manifestation, shame and honor, or a dream envisioned and a dream fulfilled? It can be a challenging time, but I want you to see the value of learning to appreciate every in-between phase of your life rather than viewing them as uneasy interruptions. I believe good things can come from every situation. Don't be overly concerned about how you got to where you are; that's not as important as savoring the moments between now and your next destination. Obviously, this is a feat much easier said than done. As I ponder my own life, I'm at least reminded that if some of my uncomfortable transitions hadn't occurred, I probably would not have some of the relationships that are so valuable to me today.

Are you feeling stuck between where you are and where you want to be? Do you have a vision of what you want your life to look like six months, one year, five years or even ten years from now? Or worse, perhaps like me, you thought that by now you'd be living the life you dreamed of ten, twenty, or even thirty years ago, but things haven't progressed the way you planned and worked hard for. Maybe you're dealing with the painful reality of where you actually are.

If you've found yourself in any of these situations, you're in the grips of a *between* period. You're dealing with an uncomfortable interlude phase in your life; and what makes it uncomfortable is that you're ready to get to some happier, more fulfilling times in your life, but you're *pressed between* some things right now. It's paramount though, that you see the wonderful possibilities in your obstacles right now. It is your God-given right to be fulfilled in your life, so learn to live with great expectation that what's ahead in your future is worth living for!

Have you ever been racing along day by day, month by month and year by year to put things in place, and then wham!, you came face to face with an obstacle, a setback, a disappointment or a tragedy? Now what do you do? I don't know the particulars of your situation, but even if I did, I wouldn't be in the position to tell you *exactly* what you should do. It is part of your own journey to search for the kind of direction you need.

What I *can* tell you is that you can't click an electronic mouse to skip over those painful periods. Nor can you rewind the videotapes of your life back to a time and place where things were more comfortable or more favorable for you. That possibility may exist in the virtual world (which no doubt many of us have grown accustomed to), but it can't happen in the real world. Life really *is* a journey, so if you're in a hurry to bypass the middle stuff, you'll miss the best lessons that only life's challenges can teach you. Trying to rush things can rob you of experiencing the wonderful elation of reaching your goals. Based on years of having to embrace those *between* phases myself, I want to offer you some time-proven suggestions that may help you.

One of the first things we must do when we get frustrated about circumstances in our lives is to accept our present truth. Embracing our reality will move us a big step closer towards gaining peace of mind. Otherwise, we can worry ourselves into a tizzy. For example, as a result of Hurricane Katrina in 2005, I was forced to leave my hometown, a place I'd returned to several years before as a place of refuge after a failed marriage. I then had to relocate to a place I didn't want to be, and the restlessness of it all almost took me down. I could no longer connect with my purpose in life, and I'd lost my rhythm. I discovered I needed to slow down my pace, get quiet on the inside and allow God to speak to my spirit. That allowed me to properly assess the situation and get back in sync with myself.

It might be helpful for you to do that, too, whenever you find yourself at one of life's uncomfortable junctures. You may be between graduating from college and facing the task of finding your first full-time job. And you're trembling at the statistics concerning the state of the economy and the increasing number of well-publicized lay-offs. *You* may even be someone who has received a pink slip recently, when a year ago you couldn't have imagined it happening to you. You may feel stuck between an abusive relationship and getting freed from it, or between a frightening medical diagnosis and renewed health. Perhaps you're between a mental breakdown and regaining your sanity. Wherever you are, know that you can get through your situation whole and not ripped apart if you give yourself permission to take all the time you need to work through it all. You have to give yourself time, though right now it may feel like time is your enemy. From experience I can tell you that if you try to rush things or rewind the video tapes of your life, you'll only set yourself up for more frustration and anxiety.

Self-Acceptance is a powerful thing. It's actually more powerful than being accepted by others, including our loved ones. When we honestly embrace where we are and who we've become, then – and only then – can we begin to find rest in our souls and can stop the inner wrestling. Recently, I spoke to a friend who had been dealing with a string of very tragic events that happened to her and her family over a three-year period. Through sobs, she told me, "I'm trying to make myself be okay." She was living in a very difficult interim period. She knew where she was emotionally, spiritually, and psychologically, and she knew where she wanted to be. However, the in-between stuff was giving her fits! My best suggestion to her was to stop trying to *make* herself be "okay." We cannot "make" ourselves be okay, when in fact we're not okay. Those efforts were counterproductive to the goal.

When we feel stuck in the interludes of our lives, we must learn to be satisfied with the *being* and not so much the *doing*. I believe that what ultimately makes us "okay" is our acceptance that, at any given moment in our lives we may *not* be okay. And there's nothing wrong with that.

Between: Getting From Where You Are To Where You Want To Be

That's why we have God. We need to lay your concerns on him. He can handle it! And often he will use others to help us through the maze of our difficult experiences. It can be truly liberating to do that.

Whenever I've found myself in a difficult phase of my own life, I, too, had the choice of either resting or wrestling. At times I've tried to wrestle away from my reality, but I found that to be too exhausting emotionally, spiritually, and physically. And I lost a lot of sleep in the process. It's when we're living through the frustration of a difficult transition that we usually question ourselves and our past life choices. Thinking we made wrong choices can perpetuate more worry and fear and often bring unfair judgment upon us. *"Why did I go to this college and not that one? Why did I marry this person, and not that one? Why did I embark on that particular business venture? Should I have chosen a different profession? Why did I move to this state? Why did I choose to delay having children or choose to not have any at all?* The questions and self-judgment seem excruciating and endless. And if we're not careful, the questions can border on the realm of the ridiculous. *Why was I born white? Why was I born black? Why wasn't I born in another country? Why was I born short? Why I wasn't born an eagle, a lion or a bear?* We just can't allow ourselves to fall prey to that.

I've learned to embrace the presence of challenges because I know that if I handle it right, it will yield great benefits for me. A lot of stuff, both good and bad, has happened between my childhood and my now, but all of those things have made me the woman I am today. I am energized when I think of my own children, for instance. They are the product of my failed first marriage. Yet, they help to direct my purpose. They are a part of one of those difficult *between* phases of my life. They're a perfect example of what I mean when I say that all things may not have always been good, but something wonderful can come from the bad times and the disappointments of life.

And we know that all things work together for good to them that love God, to them who are called according to his purpose. - Romans 8:28, KJV

Pressed Between

If you're in a chilly winter season of your life, you must remember that a lot of good things happen in the wintertime to make preparation for the spring; though it feels like everything is frozen at a standstill or at best things seem to be moving in slow motion. For instance, maybe you've sent out numerous job applications to find stable employment, but the process is taking very long. This would be the perfect time to sharpen some of the skills you will need when they do call to hire you for a position. Winter can sometimes seem long and drawn out, but it has a purpose, and purpose is everything. We shouldn't try to rush through it. Go ahead, have a good cry. Wrap up good and go for a long walk. Scream if you have to! But dare to believe that springtime is on the way and that you will fly again!

I believe that I will fly again, even though at times it feels like my wings are broken. I choose to ignore those broken wings and continue to flap them harder and harder to drown out life's debilitating messages; while allowing the positive messages to get through. I believe I will soar in the aspirations that life has been set before me. When I consider you, I am energized by the hope that is being stirred up inside of you with every page you turn in this book. I want *you* to believe in you too!

Those *between* phases just don't feel good. Each of us gets to experience numerous dips in our lifetime, which often seem to challenge us to our very souls. Who wouldn't appreciate life allowing just one setback, one disappointment, or one tragic event and having us get all of the necessary lessons for living that way? It can't happen that way. Life comes with many such experiences, and each time, we're given the opportunity to stretch and grow. But the stretching and growing can be very painful at times. In these kinds of phases, we are put in positions to reevaluate where we are. I believe that maybe God sometimes allows life to press us between some things in order to squeeze certain character flaws out of us. That's one way we can become more conformed to His image. It is in the painful interludes of our lives when we are most broken, but brokenness can be a good thing.

Just be careful not to base your self-worth on the number or intensity of the setbacks you experience. You can actually cause yourself more

9

harm if you do that. Experiencing life's challenges doesn't make you less valuable. Who told you that? Rather, if you take on a grateful attitude, these phases can turn out to be some of the most rewarding times of your life. You'll be able to say, *Thank You, God! I can see now that I needed that time in my life. I was off track and didn't realize it. I thought that everything in my life was going well, when perhaps I was only deceiving myself. I needed that breaking point.*

Feeling stuck in any of life's grueling interludes can be frustrating, aggravating, depressing, confusing and often lonely. The most aggravating part is that we don't usually get to determine how long our *between* phases will last. It could last days, weeks, months, or even years! I believe that it's determined by the purpose associated with the setback, disappointment, or trial. Sometimes we've bounced back in a short period of time, while other times, comebacks can seem to take forever. That's why it's unhealthy to compare our lives with those of others, especially when we're going through a setback that is taking us a long time from which to recover.

I'm reminded of the time right after my mother passed away. One of my colleagues at work told me that he'd *heard* somewhere that it takes approximately seven years for a person to get over the death of a loved one. That was twenty-five years ago, and I am still feeling the painful sting of that loss. When he first told me that, I remember thinking, *how can anyone determine how long someone's recovery should take?* It's not my purpose to tell you how long your current valley experience will last, but what I *would* like to do is encourage you to persevere. The sweetness of reaching your breakthrough may actually be embedded in the sourness of the process. Also, stay open to allowing your life to be a vessel of use during this time. Maybe you can even help someone else.

Your experience of living pressed between where you are and where you want to be may seem to be dragging on and on. But remember that your life is unlike anyone else's because it is *your* journey, not theirs. Perhaps you've had a house on the market for two years, and your best friend sold his or her home in thirty days. Try asking yourself what useful insights you can gain from that. It might be a stretch, but it can help to promote your own healing when you

Pressed Between

begin to embrace experiences like that as uniquely yours. Find the good in it. Maybe you've gone back to school to work on a degree and it's taking you much longer than you'd anticipated, while your colleague at work has just whisked through night school and earned a master's degree. *So what?* There is nothing wrong with you! You have to see that.

> *The sweetness of reaching your breakthrough may actually be embedded in the sourness of the process.*

We do ourselves huge disservices when we start comparing our journeys with those of other people. We all have different lessons that God is trying to teach us at these different stages of our lives. Although, more often than not, the average person is not even thinking about any lessons that God wants to teach them. That doesn't change the fact that life itself is the master teacher. Life is a school from which none of us ever really gets to graduate. There's always another lesson to be learned. Who determines which of us gets to earn a master's degree or a Ph.D. in the course of a life? Just move through your journey one day at a time. That's all that is expected of you.

Those *between* phases are when we question ourselves the most, especially when we're hurting. It can sometimes be akin to self torture. *Maybe I should have done this or maybe I should have not done that.* We can be so brutal to ourselves when we are hurting. That uncomfortable phase when we're feeling the most stuck between where we are and where we want to be is a great time to reevaluate our life choices. But it is not a time to beat up on ourselves for those times we may have erred. Turn your *betweens* into times of introspection, repentance, cleansing, healing, reflection, and planning. Remember that life doesn't present us with only one option that will render us complete failures if we blow it. Our experiences are cumulative, and we need to extract from our past experiences that which will help propel us towards more positive futures. Then, leave it at that!

11

> *That uncomfortable phase when we're feeling the most stuck between where we are and where we want to be is a great time to reevaluate our life choices. But it is not a time to beat up on ourselves for those times we may have erred.*

It is important that we take advantage of the dry seasons in our lives because it's usually then that life speaks the loudest and the clearest to us. Therefore, we must turn down the volume on all the other noise we're making. What do I mean by noise? When we spend a lot of time mumbling, complaining, kicking, or screaming about our setbacks, circumstances, and mistakes, or being too critical of ourselves, we can actually prolong the length of time of our discomfort. The children of Israel complained and grumbled in the wilderness and it caused them to spend forty years on a journey that should have taken them less than two weeks! (Deuteronomy 1:1-2). On top of that, we drown out the messages that can be heard only when we quiet down our inner selves long enough to hear.

Don't be afraid to get still for a *long* minute. The worst thing in the world is to be out of tune with oneself. Turn down the volume on all of the things that capture your attention. Stop and pray! Sometimes you may have to literally turn off the television, silence the cell phone, the Blackberry and the I-pod. Make the world wait on you this time! You need to be still so that you can hear the messages that are meant specifically for you. Don't be spooked by stillness. The clues to your next move are most likely embedded therein. Just listen.

So what should you do while in silent waiting? That's the tough part. For me, it can sometimes feel like my faith has been tested to its limit. Is it that God has shut up the heavens and refused to come down to affect my situation? Or did I miss my cue? It aches to be wedged between two uncomfortable circumstances. It can feel like you're being squeezed in the middle of your current reality and your future accomplishments. This can either immobilize or energize you, depending on your response. You may sense that you're very close to the greatest victory of your life, but you still can't touch it. Now what do you do?

I find encouragement in the scriptures because it depicts real people dealing with real life situations. It sounds like even the Psalmist was between some things when he said to God, **"But I will keep on hoping for your help; I will praise you more and more."** (Psalm 71:14.) Then, in Psalm 119: 81, it says, **"I am worn out waiting for your rescue, but I have put my hope in your word."** So, keep your head up. Put your hope in His word. Keep believing. Keep trying to find a need and meet it for someone else. And then wait, because the time is coming when things will get better for you.

So what things are you pressed between? Be careful what you place your hopes in. And seek God's wisdom concerning how you should respond to your most pressing challenges.

Here are a few *"Between"* Things

- married life and divorce court
- merely existing and discovering your life's purpose
- sickness and renewed health
- putting your house on the market and closing the sale
- ill-treatment and extending forgiveness
- job loss and career success
- the engagement party and a wedding ceremony (and you're having doubts!)
- family estrangement and reconciliation

Chapter Recap

- At any given moment in your life, you may not be "okay". And you need to become okay with that.
- Slow down to regain your rhythm.
- Don't base your self-worth on the number or intensity of your setbacks.

13

Between: Getting From Where You Are To Where You Want To Be

Questions and Thoughts to Ponder

1. If you are pressed between some things, have you found a way to encourage yourself during this time? If so, what do you do?
2. Are you concerned that it has been months (or even years), that you've been feeling stuck in the same place?
3. What has been some of the best lessons you've learned during those *between* phases of your life?

Dare to Do This

Review this chapter. Then come up with some practical ways to savor the moments of the *between* phases of your life. For example, take long, thought-filled walks. Then take notes on your thoughts!

Chapter Three

Broken

> *Often we don't realize that in some area of our lives we've been losing our footing, simply because we haven't thought about the recent rainfalls in our lives and how they may have affected the earth beneath our feet.*

I'd received a voice message from a dear friend. Her words were slow and deliberate. "Denise, you are not going to believe this. I fell down the hill and broke my ankle." I thought to myself, *What!?* I called her back to get the details. She had been working in the garden of her lovely home, lost her footing in the soft mud, and fell to the bottom of the hill! She told me that it had rained for the past three days or so, and that the earth beneath her feet was soggy. She continued, "I didn't need the hospital to tell me it was broken. I heard the bone crack!" (*Ouch!*) "That's okay," she went on. "Maybe I need to slow down anyway. Denise, I haven't taken the time to rest since Hurricane Katrina, and I haven't been reading God's word like I should."

My friend's accident forced her to realize that she'd been too busy in her life and that she'd actually been "slipping" for quite some time. "But don't worry," she assured me. "My ankle will be fine, and I will still make your wedding." You see, she was not only my close friend but

15

Between: Getting From Where You Are To Where You Want To Be

my wedding photographer as well, and I was getting remarried in three weeks! She told me that she was really determined to slow things down, and nurse her broken ankle back to health.

Isn't that how it is sometimes? We can get lost in the busyness of life, and if we're not conscientious enough, we won't realize that in some areas we've been losing our footing all along. This is because we hadn't thought about the recent rainfalls in our lives and how they may have affected the earth beneath our feet. Sometimes when we fall, we break. But, like I told my friend, we need to be "okay" with brokenness. It's when we acknowledge that something in our lives is broken that we can implement the necessary measures to aid us towards healing.

It's *easy* to pretend that there aren't any broken places in our lives. But doing that is not in our best interest. There's a bible verse that says, **"Pride goes before destruction, and haughtiness before a fall."** (Proverbs 16: 17-19). Ironically, in the end, a fall and a break can turn out to be good things, even if we don't realize it at the time we're going downhill fast!

We need to be okay with brokenness. It's when we acknowledge that something in our lives is broken that we can implement the necessary measures to aid us towards healing.

The Bible depicts David as one of the greatest Kings that have ever lived. One day he had an epiphany, and decided to discuss it with God. He said to God, **"The sacrifice you desire is a broken spirit. You will not reject a broken and repentant heart, O God."** (Psalm 51:17). It finally hit David that God was not impressed with all the great gifts of sacrifice David was bestowing upon Him. To the contrary; all God really wanted was a broken and contrite heart. That's it! We have to give God something to work with. I believe that God works best after we've been broken. It is at that moment that true healing will happen, and not a minute before. But don't worry; God is quite good at repairing broken things.

Broken

Several years ago my sister, Carolyn, called to tell me that she'd bought a new car for her youngest daughter and that I could have her old 1988 Dodge Shadow. She told me, however, that it would be my responsibility to get it fixed. That would make me its fourth owner! I gladly took on the challenge. Why not? I reasoned, *heck; wheels are better than heels!* For months, I heard strange sounds coming from underneath the hood; lots of snaps, crackles, and pops, and each time I took it in for repairs to Gerald, my friendly neighborhood "shade tree" mechanic. I got three good years out of that old Shadow!

Like my dear friend, we all need to "hear" when things in our lives break. We've all heard it said that, "if it ain't broke, don't fix it." That's good. But I say, "If it *is* broke, don't ignore it!" It may be a marriage, a career, a business gone sour, your self-esteem, or your health. I'm just saying that sometimes broken things can be fixed, so we shouldn't act like there are no problems, nor be too quick to give up on things.

I remember lying in bed one beautiful Saturday morning, several years ago; the sun was blazing outside, but it was very dark inside my room. I was going through a painful divorce and my hero (my father) had just passed away. I actually could not get up. I was too paralyzed by pain and depression. Then I heard it, almost audibly so. It sounded like a hard breadstick cracking in my chest cavity. I remember uttering these words out loud: *God, is this what a broken heart feels like?* I waited. He didn't answer; at least not then. It's been quite a few years now, and healing has visited my broken heart and confused mind. I was broken; but He touched me.

On one particular day, five years prior to that beautiful Saturday morning, I called my father crying. "Daddy, I ruined the picture!" (I had been working on a portrait of my friend). My father was a master artist and could work in any kind of medium, whether it be oils, acrylic, pen, charcoal, colored pencils, you name it. Daddy said, "Nise, (*his nickname for me*), don't worry. It's a piece of art, and art can never be ruined." I wasn't sure I believed him. He was far away on the phone. I was looking at my seemingly ruined portrait 1,100 miles away from where he sat in the comfort of his home.

I had mixed the wrong colors and applied too much pressure as I bore down on the paper with my colored pencils. At the time, I thought all I wanted to do was throw my unfinished portrait *and* my box of colored oil pencils out the back door! But my daddy convinced me otherwise. "Nise, work on the picture," he said, with a slight chuckle in his voice. "But Daddy, you don't understand!" I said between salty sobs. About a month later, I traveled to see him, my "ruined" portrait in tow. He showed me what he was trying to tell me over the phone. My portrait wasn't ruined *at all*. The grim outlook was only in my mind.

We, too, get broken and sometimes feel that we're ruined when life's trials apply the hardest pressures upon us. But remember this: we are works of art, and art can never be ruined to the point where it cannot be fixed or turned into something often more beautiful. Speaking of art, God is the *master* potter, and He knows how to put broken things back together again. Listen to this. **"The Lord gave another message to Jeremiah. He said, 'Go down to the potter's shop and I will speak to you there.' So I did as he told me and found the potter working at his wheel. But the jar he was making did not turn out as he had hoped, so he crushed it into a lump of clay again and started over. Then the Lord gave me this message. 'O Israel, can I not do to you as the potter has done to his clay? As the clay is in the potter's hand, so are you in my hand.'"** (Jeremiah 18: 1-6). Okay, so maybe yours is a broken dream or a broken heart. Well, don't fret about it because broken things can heal and sometimes turn out better than the original, when it's all said and done.

> *We've all heard it said that, "if it ain't broke, don't fix it." I say, "If it is broke, don't ignore it!" It may be a marriage, a career, a business gone sour, your self-esteem, or your health. I'm just saying that sometimes broken things can be fixed, so we shouldn't act like there are no problems, nor be too quick to give up on things.*

Well, my friend nursed her broken ankle, and it did heal in time for her to take her role as my wedding photographer three weeks later! The

Broken

portrait of my other friend turned out to be a priceless gift to her, even though I had to work very hard to make that happen. Just as well, the broken places and things in your life can turn out to be better than you could have ever imagined if you believe, don't give up, and work hard at it. Remember, whatever it is, give it to God in prayer. He specializes in fixing broken things.

Chapter Recap

- Sometimes we lose our footing without realizing that we've been slipping all along.
- We need to be okay with brokenness. It is when we acknowledge that something in our lives is broken that we can implement the necessary measures to aid us towards healing.
- Never give up! Keep believing! Work hard!

Questions and Thoughts to Ponder

1. Have you been ignoring the cracking, snapping and popping sounds of the broken places in your life?
2. What areas of your life do you think might be ruined or broken beyond repair?
3. Are you okay with brokenness?

Dare To Do This

Pick up the broken pieces of the areas of your life, which you'd otherwise like to toss out the back door, (as I wanted to do with my unfinished portrait). Believe that it can be repaired. Then take it to the *master potter* (God), and let Him fix it.

Chapter Four

You Don't Have to Fear the Stuff in the Middle

> *Become so wrapped up in something, you forget to be afraid. — Lady Bird Johnson*

Have you ever been caught in the grips of fear? I have. Fear can be debilitating. You may be wedged between some things right now, but try not to let the harsh stuff interrupt your living. Imagine this: you've put your dreams out there. Now others know about the goals you've set out to reach. Some people in your life will doubt you. Some will discourage you. Others may even try to hinder you. But it's always good to consider the source of all of this negative energy.

Determine to never allow fear of anything or anyone keep you from setting goals, or from taking advantage of great opportunities. I did that on more than a few occasions, and let me tell you, it leads only to sorrowful regrets. When you look back over your life and see the times you failed to make good on an opportunity, you will probably find that a spirit of fear was lurking around you and held you back.

At times, though, it's the people who are paralyzed by their *own* fears who can't accept others taking the plunge towards reaching their unique goals. For the most part, of course, the people in our lives mean well, but if we aren't careful, we'll allow them to inadvertently transfer their fears onto us. The thing to do in situations like this is to love those

You Don't Have to Fear the Stuff in the Middle

people anyway, and assure them that you're following your heart, have calculated all of the known risks involved, and will not shy away from those unknown.

I remember the day I turned forty years old. One of my older brothers came by my house and said, "Look at you, you're all washed up. All you do is spend time with your children and hang out with them at the library and stuff. You need to be going out to the clubs to party. What man is going to want you, especially with two children?" Initially, I felt crushed. But then I put things in perspective. I could not figure out what was wrong with my decision to spend the best part of my days with my children, investing in their lives, spending quality time with them, getting to know them, etc. I did not think it wise to invest my time on the hunt for a new man, as my brother thought I should. I believed that things would work out in the end, if I put my priorities first and stayed on a spiritual path.

My brother really didn't mean me any harm. He loves me and my children. That was just his take on life. I later told him that it was a good thing that I had a healthy self-esteem at the time or else his comments would have taken me down. (Actually, I really was *struggling* to keep my self-esteem intact following a devastating divorce, the loss of my home, my career, and the recent death of our father). My response to his remarks was to press on with a fierce ambition to improve my life.

My brother, then 57, eventually admitted he'd felt that *his* life was "washed up" when *he* turned forty. You see, it's important that we not allow other people's mindsets or perspectives to color how we feel about things when we know that we have strong goals and a bright vision for our future. We may have to hold on to our visions for dear life, but so be it, if that is what's necessary to move towards accomplishing our dreams. There's something on the inside of us that won't let us rest until we've at least given our ideas, goals, and visions a determined and persistent chance to blossom. Incidentally, about one year later, I met my current husband at church, and that particular brother of mine had to eat his words! He later told to me that I had a "good man."

Now, let's say that you've already lovingly responded to your "no vision" friends and family members concerning your decision to step out and dare to make a positive imprint in the world, or improve your

21

Between: Getting From Where You Are To Where You Want To Be

life in some way. What about the other critics who will inevitably show up? You have to be so in touch with yourself and your dream that you'll have an answer for anyone who tries to thwart you. However, be assured that your answer need not be in words but more powerfully in your persistent commitment to work hard at realizing your goals and seeing your dreams come to pass. That's the most effective way to shut the lion's mouth!

I found out, though, that the biggest and worst critic we will ever have to face is the one who resides inside our own heads. That's the big boy of all of our enemies! To that I say, talk to yourself about your dreams and goals. Brainstorm ways you can silence your own worst critic, the one that screams at you from the inside. Say positive things about yourself, to yourself, when the going gets tough. Coach yourself, and cheer yourself on! Write your goals down. Then put them all over your house if you have to. See yourself as the victor and no longer the victim of fear, inaction, immaturity, mental fatigue, negativity, or doubt.

Another key to reaching your goals or coming out of whatever negative circumstances you find yourself in is to stay enthusiastic! Even in the midst of the many simultaneous trials and setbacks I was dealing with, I remained hopeful. I was able to maintain an optimistic outlook because I knew my setbacks were not the end of my story. There was no period there, only a comma, and through God, I had within me the power to turn things around. And I certainly expected to do just that!

Hope is a powerful thing. And if hope is effective enough to lead us to eternal life, then certainly it can help us with the battles we face in our earthly journeys. Listen to what Romans 5:3-5a tells us. **"We can rejoice, too, when we run into problems and trials, for we know that they help us develop endurance. And endurance develops strength of character, and character strengthens our confident hope of salvation. And this hope will not lead to disappointment."**

My hope is that by now you, too, are getting excited about seeing positive things happen in your life. When we're optimistic and are willing to work hard and cooperate with the plan of God to achieve our goals, we don't have to fear everything we're sure to encounter in the middle. Are you wondering whether or not you'll experience difficulties

You Don't Have to Fear the Stuff in the Middle

on your way to reaching your goals? Certainly you will. Will you encounter setbacks and disappointments? Absolutely! But don't sweat it. It's all a part of the middle experience on the way to achieving great things. And you can count on more than a few naysayers getting in your business. People may start untrue rumors about you. Don't chase after those rumors, because pursuing them is a huge waste of your time and resources. Your energy is best used on your vision of a better life. There will be all sorts of drama, setbacks, foolishness, personal mistakes, and unfair treatment. Things like that will inevitably occur on the way from where you are to where you want to be. And even if fear does rear its ugly head in your life, be unwavering, and go forth anyway, one step at a time!

Usually, life doesn't offer short cuts. We all know from seventh grade geometry that the shortest distance between two points is a straight line. But we don't usually get to experience life in straight lines. Wouldn't it be wonderful if we could? Life doesn't occur in perfect 90 degree right angles either. Mostly, we experience it in ways that mostly resemble random curves, parabolas, and zigzags!

Discover what's between you and the fulfillment of your goals, and perhaps making the greatest contribution you could ever make in your life. But just know that it doesn't really matter what's in the middle. You can push through any obstacle or setback if your goals are strong enough and you're being lead by the Spirit of God. Find some noble endeavor that you can "become so wrapped up in" that you'll actually forget about being afraid of all the stuff in the middle. Muster up the courage to at least start where you are.

> *Nothing is as necessary for success as the single-minded pursuit of an objective. – Fred Smith, (founder and CEO of Federal Express)*

For many of you, just starting will itself be a great motivator. Take it one day at a time, pace yourself, and know that you're on the right track because you're keeping your eyes on the prize. You are here, but you

Between: Getting From Where You Are To Where You Want To Be

want to be there. Make up your mind that you'll at least try to embrace the reality of everything else in- between, even the stuff that scares you or that doesn't feel good. Keep telling yourself that something good can come from it anyway. Learn to live life with deliberate purpose, and discover ways to appreciate those many transitions on the way to where you hope to be. Welcome to your own journey!

Chapter Recap

1. Whenever you set out to make a positive decision in your life, you can expect to encounter setbacks, disappointments and heartache.
2. You don't have to fear the stuff in the middle; it's all a part of your journey to getting where you need to be.
3. Don't allow others to transfer their fears on to you.
4. Push hard through the hard times!

Questions and Thoughts to Ponder

1. What real setbacks have you encountered on your way to reaching your goals?
2. What *imagined* fears have kept you paralyzed in the same position?
3. Have you been chasing after someone else's negative rumors about you, by trying to defend yourself? It's not worth your time, because doing so can hinder your progress.

Dare To Do This

Imagine that you've been interviewed by your favorite magazine about your best accomplishments. What would the article say? Use your creative imagination to write the article yourself, as if you've already achieved your highest and best! Post it, and refer to it often for inspiration and motivation.

Chapter Five

Mistakes, Messes and Miracles

> *I can now say that I appreciate every mistake I've made and every mess I've ever gotten myself into because they make me hopeful that miracles can come from them.*

Which of us has not been disappointed with ourselves at one time or another? A mistake is an error that is often based on a misunderstanding or a lack of judgment. We've all heard it said many times that everyone makes mistakes. It's just that when we're that someone who errs, the sting of it can be extremely painful.

If we're not careful, though, we can begin to sink in our own estimation of ourselves because we fail to see particular mistakes on the backdrop of the entire canvas of our lives. That is what God would do. Also, unlike the creator, we tend to not separate who we are, from the mistakes we've made. I'm sure that when you first read the title of this chapter, your mind began to automatically rewind the tapes of your life to playback every one of your blunders from birth until now. Just remember, those videotapes never take into account the bright future that's in store for you. In fact, if it were possible to get a mental image of all of your future possibilities, then your past mistakes would wane in comparison to all the good things up ahead.

Between: Getting From Where You Are To Where You Want To Be

Here's a quote I love by Lord Anton: "Imagine a congress of eminent celebrities such as More, Bacon, Grotius, Pascal, Cromwell, Bossuet, Montesquieu, Jefferson, Napoleon, Pitt, etc. There would be an encyclopedia of errors." In other words, we need to keep our thoughts in perspective. These notable people would cringe at the thought that perhaps others might perceive them as those who've made little or no major mistakes in their lives. Their successes have not been determined by how few mistakes they made but rather by the fact that, in spite of how much they erred, they faced it and moved forward.

> *Here's to the past. Thank God it's past!*
> *– Unknown*

In the biblical book, Philippians, the apostle Paul tells us the advantage of letting the past be past. According to him, we should **"forget those things which are behind and press on."** (Philippians 1:13b, KJV). I agree with him one hundred percent! Allowing our mistakes to torment us is counterproductive and can hinder our progress, so why expend our energies there?

You may argue that your mistakes were so huge that it caused you to lose your job or your career. Perhaps your mistakes contributed to the demise of your marriage, or maybe it caused tremendous pain to another family or another individual. Contrary to all the negative thoughts that penetrate your mind, your mistakes can never disqualify you in the all encompassing journey of life. Rather, with the proper perspective, they can have the opposite effect; that is, qualify you to have a great impact on the world.

Guilt, like fear, can be debilitating too. Just beware, that sometimes you can experience a false sense of guilt. Perhaps you've carried a false guilt that you're responsible for some abuse that was done to you in your childhood. You may think, if only you hadn't been there, or if only you hadn't been such a bad boy or girl, or if only you hadn't looked so much like your dad, then maybe your mom wouldn't have beat you so much. Learn to separate who you are from the abuse you endured because of

Mistakes, Messes and Miracles

perverted individuals who were in authority over you, or adults that chose to violate your innocence. They were the perpetrators, not you. You should never blame yourself for their wrongdoings. You are still precious in God's sight.

Perhaps your guilt is real. By that, I mean that maybe *you* were the person who did wrong. Maybe you stole from your employer, and it cost you your job. Maybe you forgot a pot of boiling water on the stove, and your toddler climbed up, tipped it over, and suffered severe burns. Whatever the guilt may be, you need to give yourself time and space to work through it. There's something very liberating about confession. You might just need to remind yourself that it was an error in judgment or an accident, knowing full well that otherwise you would've never caused any harm to another person. Did you make the mistake of sharing another person's confidences, and the information spread like wildfire through your workplace, church, or synagogue, causing severe hurt to the person and a breach in your relationship with them? All you can do is offer an acknowledgment of the wrongdoing, followed by a sincere apology. Then get the lessons from it, and move towards personal healing.

William D. Brown said, "Failure is an event, not a person." I once saw a story on television which featured a young man who had accidentally killed a mother and her young daughter while drag racing down a city block. The van they were riding in exploded into a ball of fire upon impact. The young man, along with the husband and father of the deceased, now travel all over the country speaking to students about the dangers of drag racing. He is probably still feeling a strong sense of guilt over having caused so much pain to that family, and perhaps his own, but he has chosen to give back to the community in the only way he knows how.

Hopefully, through that experience, he's learned that his mistake is something that happened. It is *not* who he is. And I cannot help but respect the husband, who could have otherwise chosen to be unforgiving towards that young man, to his *own* detriment. But instead, he chose to look outside of himself and embrace the young man who took his family away from him because he knew that man was hurting deeply, too. Being able to travel around the country with that young man has to in some way have brought at least a semblance of healing to the

27

Between: Getting From Where You Are To Where You Want To Be

husband. He has taken his pain and used it as a catalyst to prevent other young people from engaging in dangerous behaviors that could possibly take the lives of other innocent people. God can still turn our mistakes, messes, and maladies into miracles, but only if we're willing to let Him use us. Of course, the larger lesson in this story is the husband's willingness to forgive, which I think opened the way for him to view his tragedy objectively.

> *Failure is an event, not a person*
> *— William D. Brown*

Maybe you don't know how to turn your tragedy, personal pain, or guilt into a crusade to help others. Trust your heart! Then share with a trusted friend, therapist, pastor, or rabbi that you'd like to give back in some way to help others with their pains even though you are still working through your very own. Don't feel like you have to do something grand. Perhaps it's volunteering at a homeless shelter, mentoring youth, or making homemade crafts or cards to send to our troops overseas. Whatever it is, there's a ministry inside of you!

Sometimes our pain moves us towards our purpose and passion. Life doesn't allow us to stop at the pain, but it will present many opportunities for healing through giving back if we're attentive enough to hear the cues. Recovery is a journey, and once we embrace that as fact, we won't have to wait until we're completely healed to bless others. We can start now because our darkest hour can provide light to someone else in his or her time of need. Yes, I truly believe that our mistakes, messes and maladies can be turned into miracles, and we get to decide.

> *Sometimes a noble failure serves the world as faithfully as a distinguished success — Dowden.*

28

Mistakes, Messes and Miracles

Chapter Recap

- Guilt can sometimes be real, but often, it's imagined, and it can cause people to take on responsibilities that are not theirs.
- Don't take responsibility for someone else's life choices, especially those of other adults.
- Any mistake, mess, or malady can be turned into a miracle of service to others.

Questions to Ponder

1. Do you think that we get our greatest lessons from our mistakes or from our successes? Explain your answer.
2. If you find yourself in a mess right now, how important do you think acceptance is in moving towards turning it into a miracle?
3. Can any good come from self-condemnation? How can it actually hinder us from moving to a positive and productive place?

Dare To Do This

You don't have to do something grand in order to turn your mistakes into miracles. I challenge you to commit yourself to doing something that will turn just one of your mistakes into a miracle.

Chapter Six

Shame, Shame, Shame

> *Facing it – always facing it – that's the way to get through it. Face it! -Joseph Conrad*

What is one thing that you've done right in your life? Perhaps right now that's your one string, so play it. It's bound to bring forth a new melody from within your soul. Life often seems to illuminate our faults more readily than it does our goodness, so it can easily feel like a battle when we try to hold on to perhaps that one good thing about ourselves. Indeed, it *is* a battle. You see, it's easier to feel defeated than to feel a sense of accomplishment in the midst of a temporary defeat. That's one thing we must work very hard to guard against.

I'm reminded of that popular song from the early 1990's, "Always Something There to Remind Me." Do you know what I've learned about feelings of shame and disgrace? You just have to face them. Our father used to have a saying when my siblings and I would leave the house. He'd say, "Okay, don't disgrace the name." There was just something special about being a Lewis. I've had personal and moral failures and have made many mistakes in my life, but whenever my mind is inundated with the shameful reminders of those blunders, I remind myself that I'm still accepted by God, **"To the praise of the glory of his grace, wherein he hath made us accepted in the beloved.**

30

In whom we have redemption through his blood, the forgiveness of sins, according to the riches of his grace."** (Ephesians 1: 6-7, KJV). Let me tell you, it's a huge weight lifter.

I have to continue talking to myself on this issue. I say over and over again, out loud, "I may have made some mistakes, but I have nothing of which to be ashamed." There's a fine line between self-examination and self-condemnation; therefore, be careful to not judge yourself too harshly. Of course, we all should examine ourselves to see if we are still moving in an upward direction. But thank God that the condemnation factor has been removed! **"There is now no condemnation to them which are in Christ Jesus, who walk not after the flesh, but after the Spirit."** (Romans 8:1, KJV). My admonition to you is that you continue to walk in the Spirit. Life encompasses a string of mistakes and alarming transitions, but one can always begin again. Approach your mistakes with honesty but remain open to gaining the lessons from those experiences. Allow the Word and Spirit of God to be that "something" that is *always there* to remind you of your great worth.

What is one thing that you've done right in your life? Perhaps right now that's your one string, so play it. It's bound to eventually bring forth a new melody from within your soul.

Sometimes, our biggest temptation is to run from feelings of shame, but whatever we do, we must not run. Some of you are buried underneath a mountain of shame. I have been there, and the easiest thing to do is to wish that a big rock would just crush us during those times, but instead, we must learn to hide behind *the* Rock. Or like one of my favorite hymns says; *Rock of ages, cleft for me, let me hide myself in thee.* We ought to let God be that rock that holds us up steadily. He cannot be moved.

I've also found it helpful to try to discern the reason behind the shame. Sometimes we tend to nurture feelings of shame that aren't ours

Between: Getting From Where You Are To Where You Want To Be

in the first place. We should consider the things or situations from our past, or present, that may be the source of our feelings of shame and then discover what we can do now to bring down that wall of shame and self-loathing.

So what is your shame? Are you ashamed that you didn't complete your formal education? Then consider looking for a way to go back to school to improve your life in that way. You may have to take one class at a time, at night, or online, but at least it's a start. Often, it's only after you've begun a task that you gain momentum. Are you ashamed of the type of relationships you've embraced over the years? Well, in that, too, you can switch course. Don't be so desperate that you would settle for any kind of relationship. You are too precious for that. I'll say that in another way. You are valuable! God loves you. You don't need another human being to validate your worth.

If there's someone in your life who's sapping your energy and demeaning you, then you must find a way to disarm him or her. Notice, I did not say to fight him or her. I said you need to *disarm* him or her. Stop giving that person your power. Gird yourself up and realize that you can speak up for yourself. Ask God to give you wisdom and strength to remove yourself from relationships that tear you down rather than build you up. Sometimes it may be a matter of drawing the line and informing another individual that you will no longer tolerate disregard and disrespect from him or her. It's not only okay, but often necessary to sever relationships that cause you to sink deeper into feelings of shame.

If your shame is caused by some of your own mistakes or life choices, to that I gingerly say, so what? I remember feeling so bad about one of my failings that I just walked and walked all day long in a park. My mind was in a confused panic. I felt my spirit was disconnected from God's, and I just wanted to turn back the clock. However, it was too late for that. I felt washed up, useless, and empty, but I needed to accept my failure and move beyond. I needed to be sure deep down within that my story just couldn't end like that. I knew I still had value. Besides, I had two children on whom to concentrate. They needed me. I *couldn't* quit. Well, I guess I could have, but who would have taken care of them? All I could see at the moment was

32

Shame, Shame, Shame

me, but I needed to get outside of myself as soon as possible and see their needs.

Then I told myself that I still had things to accomplish, and that I hadn't reached my plateau yet, in terms of my overall success in life. Additionally, I thought I'd lost the right to write and speak to inspire others after I'd experienced so much failure. After all, I reasoned, *don't I have a failed marriage, a lost career, a depleted sense of self-worth, a food stamp card and an empty bank account?* I thought that the accumulation of setbacks, disappointments, and personal mistakes had disqualified me. But following many months of quiet reflection, I resumed reaching out to others through teaching and speaking again. Eventually, as I continued to uplift others, I got my rhythm back, and I realized that I was no different from anyone else who'd experienced some failures.

I still had a lot to contribute, but I needed to regroup, refocus and regain responsibility for the goals I'd set for myself. It may seem quite audacious to believe that the world would be a better place if we would make our positive contributions, no matter the size, but that is the reality. The world *would* be better off with our contributions.

Sadly, I also remember a time in my life when I allowed shame to cause me to build a wall of separation in my relationships with loving and caring friends. Several of my friends called from out of state to track me down. One friend told me, "Denise, do you really think that you can run away?" Another friend was so determined to get in touch with me that she even called the private school my children were attending at the time and asked to speak to the headmaster of the school. I was even more embarrassed when he called to tell me that he had spoken to her. He told me that she had been really concerned about me and my children, and that I really needed to call her. I did. But I really didn't want to talk to any of my friends. I just felt that they deserved more than I could offer them at the time, and I just wanted a place to bury my head. Shame can cause us to do unwise things. I had suffered a few big disappointments, but so what? I just thank God that I had friends who cared enough to shake me out of my foolish stupor!

My decision to hide from my well-meaning friends only brought more shame upon me. I guess I was just having an extended off-

33

Between: Getting From Where You Are To Where You Want To Be

season, and I'd convinced myself that I wanted to be left alone to press through my crises. Shame, shame, shame on me! You see, up until that time, my life had been virtually carefree and I'd experienced very few disappointments and setbacks. Suddenly, I was hit on every side, with back to back challenges, and I was losing my footing.

Another friend later told me that she couldn't find my telephone number, which I'd changed twice, so she asked a co-worker to help her to search online for anyone who lived in my neighborhood in New Orleans, a city with which she was unfamiliar. I found out a few years later that, in fact, she had spoken to my next-door neighbor, (who'd known me since birth)! Unfortunately, he was an elderly man with health issues, and who died suddenly of a heart attack before he remembered to tell me that my friend had called his home. I allowed my shame to keep me away from people who I knew loved me and my children. Again, shame on me!

I thought I'd let myself down and that I had to get myself together first before contacting my friends again. I felt that most of my friends were very successful in their lives, careers, marriages, and finances. And I thought I should have been, too. Shame is a wicked thing, and if we nurture it, it can incapacitate us, cause us to do foolish things, and make us ineffective in life.

I had allowed myself to drop out of the race, and I knew that somehow I had to muster up the courage to get back in. One friend later told me that I had nothing to be ashamed of. He reminded me that as a single mother I'd achieved so many things and had kept my children loved, well cared for and surrounded by good people. He commented on how well-mannered, spiritually balanced and academically successful my children were, even through the many transitions that plagued us. He helped me to see that I had a lot to be proud of. I learned to keep reminding myself that my journey to success was uniquely mine. I soon began to realize that all I had experienced was all a part of God's larger plan to get me closer to accomplishing great things in life. As a result of all this, I started saying aloud to myself, "I have nothing of which to be ashamed".

In your situation, you'll just have to be bold in your thinking too, or else you'll have no need of an enemy because you will have defeated

34

yourself. You must imagine yourself being a blessing to your church, a neighbor, a long forgotten acquaintance, or someone halfway across the world from you. It can sometimes feel like a mind game, but it's a game you can win.

One game you cannot afford to play is the blame game. The words "if only" may be very familiar to you. If only you'd done this or that, or not done this or that. If only your husband or wife had treated you differently, then perhaps you wouldn't have gotten a divorce. If only you had spent less time at work and more time at home. If only. Don't beat yourself up with the "what ifs" and the "if onlys." Take hold of your thoughts. Life happens. Take responsibility where appropriate but that is where it should stop. Otherwise, those thoughts will energize your feelings of shame, and there's no place in your journey for that.

During the times when you have the tendency to judge yourself unfairly, try instead, to focus on your recovery and healing. Don't dwell too long on why something happened, but rather focus on how you can positively respond to it in such a way that one good thing can come from the experience. Blaming yourself or others for your shame can make you bitter and can actually prolong your healing and recovery, and prevent you from getting to the place of feeling powerful.

> *Don't beat yourself up with the "what ifs" and the "if onlys." Take hold of your thoughts. Life happens. Take responsibility where appropriate but that is where it should stop.*

What mistakes or life choices are you ashamed of? Please don't do what I did. Don't run from the shame. No, I didn't run away physically, but I ran away spiritually and emotionally, which was worse. Face whatever it is. Your life is still very useful! Fortunately for me, eventually, I went to God with my shame and He showed me that I was still valuable to Him. Then one day I picked up my bible and for a reason that I don't remember, I started reading the book of Philemon, and realized that in many ways, I was like the main character in the story. I put together a bible teaching based on the story, because reading it had helped me tremendously. Sometime later, I had an opportunity to present that teaching to my church. I called it, "Useful Runaways." It highlights the life story of a runaway slave named Onesimus, who ran from his master whom he'd wronged. (Some theologians think that Onesimus had stolen from Philemon). Unbeknownst to Onesimus, he would come face to face with the apostle Paul, who cared enough about Onesimus to help him recognize his self-worth. And I can only image how grateful he must have been to Paul.

Paul wrote a very compelling letter to Onesimus' master, who was his good friend Philemon. On Onesimus' behalf, Paul wrote, **"I appeal to you to show kindness to my child, Onesimus. I became his father in the faith while here in prison. Onesimus *hasn't been of much use to you in the past, but now he is very useful* to both of us. (Italics mine). I am sending him back to you, and with him comes my own heart. It seems that Onesimus ran away for a little while so that you could have him back forever."** (Philemon 1: 10-12, 15). That is a very powerful statement! Like Onesimus, our shame (or fear) may cause us to run away from something, but it should be only for a "little while" so that we can give ourselves back to our life's purpose, "forever"! This story had an incredible impact on my self-esteem. The name Onesimus actually means "useful." It took me a while, but I realized that I, too, was a "useful runaway." I needed to be of use to the world, but I couldn't do that if I allowed myself to run away and shut down.

Do you think you've wronged the Master? Perhaps you've run away from God because of fear or shame. Run back to Him! You are still very useful! Give yourself back to His will and purpose for your life, "forever". Never allow your shame to hold you back from going beyond where you are. Your story is not over yet! William Arthur Ward said, "Failure is delay, but not defeat. It is a temporary detour, not a dead-end street." You can't afford to let your journey end on such a note. You have within you the power to write the ending to your own story. It's your script. Do with it whatever you want to!

> *Failure is delay, but not defeat. It is a temporary detour,*
> *not a dead-end street. - William Arthur Ward*

There should be no lingering shame in your life. Remind yourself that, like the weather, life moves in cycles and seasons. You might be going through a season of shame now, but know that that's okay and that you *will* come out of it. Your job is to decide where you want to go from where you are. If you don't know the answer to that, don't panic. I suggest purchasing a journal or notebook and just start writing. You may say at first, "but, I'm not a writer". You don't have to be a writer to write. Simply write everything that you're thinking or feeling. Don't edit anything! It's just your own thoughts, so you don't need to be afraid of them, and you certainly should not judge them. Just write!

Something will eventually surface to the top, perhaps an idea, a goal, or a longing. If it's something you would've never considered doing in the past, or a career path or life choice you could've never imagined before, that's okay, too. Go with the flow of your thoughts. Maybe an idea will keep coming up that might cause you to have to switch directions in a life-changing way. It might put you in the company of people you would've never thought about working with before. Start embracing that as a possibility.

Even if you're in a mental funk, write about it. I've been there, too, countless times. Imagine yourself coming out on the other side of where you find yourself now. Recognize that everyone errs. You will see your mistakes in a different light once you deal with the shame factor. Of course, though, while you're experiencing shameful and humiliating *between* phases, you're not always going to see it that way. Feelings of shame and humiliation can be some of the hardest to overcome, but it can be done. I am telling you what I know.

Right about now you may be thinking, "But Denise, you've already come through your tough times." I've got to tell you that nothing could be further from the truth. I had a tough decision to make about my shame. I just had to decide that I was either going to allow it to cause

Between: Getting From Where You Are To Where You Want To Be

me to fold or allow it to light a flame underneath me and cause me to move closer to what I believe is my God-ordained life purpose. I don't believe I would be qualified to ask something of you that I'm not doing myself or have never had to do.

I've become an expert at beginning again because I've had to start over many times from scratch. Life will always afford you the option of starting over again from where you are. Sure, it might feel like you're behind everyone else, but you have to find your own pace and your own rhythm. You're not a part of a robotic nation, so you don't have to do what the masses are doing. Go according to the course God has charted specifically for you. Though I've had to start over many times, I'm very hopeful, and I've chosen to stand up in my expectation that better things are on the horizon for me. I'm writing this book with you in mind. You are hurting, and I want to offer you the hope that I have. I'm sensing my own healing with each word of encouragement I give to you, the reader. I see you coming out of your slump, when the time is right, but I also see you reaching out to be of service to others in your own way.

The *size* of your gesture isn't important; what *is* important is that whatever you give or share, do it with a compassionate heart. I've chosen to use my gift of writing to encourage you. So, we're making this journey together. I'm convinced that the best remedy for our own shame is to stand up, dust off, begin again, and then reach out to help someone else. I find no shame in that!

> *Instead of shame and dishonor, you will enjoy a double share of honor (Psalm 61: 7).*

Chapter Recap

- Your shame may be caused by something you've done or failed to do. Either way, don't sweat yourself about it.
- It may feel like the easiest thing to do is to run from your feelings of shame, but whatever you do, don't run. Face whatever it is.

- Don't play the blame game.
- You can always begin again!

Questions and Thoughts to Ponder

1. In what way has your loss or mistake made you feel ashamed?
2. Some shame is real, but more often than not, it's imagined. Can you tell the difference?
3. Have you ever been too ashamed to let even your closest confidantes know that you're experiencing a season of shame? Did you finally make the decision to share your feelings with them? If so, what made you come to that decision? If not, what held you back from sharing?

Dare To Do This

Make some kind of physical reminder of at least one positive thing that you've done in your life. It can be a placard, a laminated card to carry in your wallet, a poem, etc. Make sure to keep it in plain view to help you to stay encouraged.

Chapter Seven

A Window of Time and a Door of Opportunity

> *Opportunity beckons more surely when misfortune comes upon a person than it ever does when that person is riding the crest of a wave of success.*
> *– Earl Nightingale*

Have you ever considered that your window of time might be situated directly across the hallway from your door of opportunity? We all need time to heal and recover following devastating losses, whatever those losses may be. I, for instance, firmly believe that following a romantic breakup or divorce, one should take time to heal and regroup before rushing off into another relationship. I'm also convinced that when we're at our lowest points and think we have nothing to give, we are then in the best position *to* give. If we think otherwise, we may be making a huge mistake. Trust me, we may think our present situation is awful, but there is always someone, somewhere, who could benefit from something we could share to raise him or her up a little. If we would but step outside of ourselves for just a little while, we'll soon discover that in our deepest pain, we can provide light to other hurting souls. Our most pressing pain can become our most perfect pain, to benefit others, and even ourselves, depending on how we use it.

A Window of Time and a Door of Opportunity

Right now, I'm thinking about a mother who lost her daughter to a car accident caused by a drunk driver, yet she turned outward instead of turning inward. Cindy Lightner embraced the opportunity to use her pain as a catalyst to launch a campaign aimed at preventing or at least slowing down the rate at which so many innocent people are killed by intoxicated drivers every year. I am sure that Mrs. Lightner was broken-hearted and angry, but she directed that anger in such a way as to positively affect society. Of course she was mad, but she decided to make something good come from that tragedy. Mrs. Lightner is still "MADD," which is why there's a MADD (Mothers Against Drunk Drivers) chapter in just about every state in America and also in locations abroad. A couple of years ago I heard her speak at a women's conference, and she had to fight back tears as she approached yet another anniversary of her daughter's tragic death. Through her pain, she made the courageous decision to walk through her door of opportunity to make a great contribution.

Your loss may be of a different kind, such as the loss of a job, a home, or business. Maybe the loss of your job or career will give you ideas to start your own business venture, or give you the incentive to go after an even better career opportunity. Perhaps the loss of a home will be a catalyst for you to finally get a handle on your spending habits and get your finances in order. I've known people who, following a job loss, have invested in themselves by going back to school to study a totally different field from what they've been accustomed to working in as a career. All of these examples can be viewed as windows of opportunity for making good on losses and disappointments.

My point here is to convince you that you don't have to wait until you've got all the answers before you can make positive investments in your life, the life of another individual, or in your community. This is your door of opportunity! You don't have to wait until you know what you're going to do about your house, your estate, your career, or your broken self-esteem. Look beyond your current situation, and look for opportunities that present themselves to you. What I can almost guarantee you, is that as you look outside yourself to meet another person's need, you will begin to receive your own inner healing.

Between: Getting From Where You Are To Where You Want To Be

There is something very powerful about giving, because it's based on an eternal principle. "Give and you will receive. Your gift will return to you in full, pressed down, shaken together to make room for more, running over, and poured into your lap. The amount you give will determine the amount you get back" (Luke 6:38). Give comfort to another, and in some way, you will receive comfort in return. Give friendship, and you will be befriended in your time of need. Give encouragement, and your soul will be encouraged in return. Albert Schweitzer said, "You don't live in a world all your own. Your brothers are here, too."

> *You don't have to wait until you've got all the answers before you can make positive investments in your life, the life of another individual, or in your community. You don't have to wait until you know what you're going to do about your house, your estate, your career, or your broken self-esteem.*

The easiest thing to do is to try to talk your way out of this powerful principle of giving. Don't worry that you may not be qualified enough. That thought has no essence for you. *Life* has qualified you. I went through a phase when I thought my mistakes and poor life choices had disqualified me, but nothing could have been further from the truth. Additionally, I worried about what people might think or say about me. I thought I wasn't pretty enough or educated enough or that I didn't have the "right connections." After all, I reasoned, *what do I have to give?* I wondered if I could really make a powerful contribution.

There may be times when you know you've given all you can give to attain your goals or to come out of your slump, and you feel absolutely spent. My advice to you is to keep giving, and stretching, and planning, and implementing, and hoping. Consistency and perseverance will win out every time. You have to keep faith that things will get better. You don't know what might be right around the corner for you. Your breakthrough moment may be just over the hump, so you should be

42

looking for that door of opportunity. You should literally be expecting it because it will surely open itself to you.

Just remember that when your door of opportunity does present itself, you must be ready to walk through it! Don't worry that you might not have everything in perfect order. Just go through that door, and believe that divine guidance will be yours every step of the way. Believe that your steps are ordered by God, and if He opens a door for you, then He obviously believes you are deserving of it. So make good on it! Believe in yourself. It doesn't matter if you've been told most of your life that your input is not important, and it doesn't matter that you struggle with feelings of self-doubt. Thank God that the past is over with, and that this is a new day for you, with a new slate, a new faith, and a new boldness and tenacity for living!

> *Don't worry that you might not have everything in perfect order. Just go through that door of opportunity, and believe that divine guidance will be yours every step of the way.*

I am on a mission to encourage you, to uplift you, and to get you to see how valuable you are to this world. Hold on. Don't quit. You may be crawling now, but still, don't quit. You may be walking with a limp, but don't quit! You may be nursing a broken heart. You may be broken in spirit, but whatever you do, just don't quit. Cry out to God! He hears, and He answers prayers! He has something for you to do. You are valuable in ways you have never imagined. Doors of opportunity will open to you, but you must be committed to staying the course and giving, and giving, and giving, especially when you don't feel like doing so. Giving will come back to you twenty, thirty, and even one hundred fold. It'll be a win-win situation.

Life can be so deceptive at times because it can make you think that everyone else's life is perfect and only yours is a mess. (I cannot begin to tell you how many times I thought that). But, believe it or not, you're surrounded by wounded people all of the time. You just may

43

Between: Getting From Where You Are To Where You Want To Be

not be in tune with it. Perhaps you're thinking about a colleague who seems to have it all together. That person might be suffering from a loss of self-esteem, some other major loss, or they might be on the verge of a mental breakdown. Life isn't supposed to revolve around you. That's why I believe that, even in the midst of your pain, you should seek to reach out to someone who may be hurting deeply as well.

Not long after Hurricane Katrina, I was asked to give a keynote address about my experience, and at first, I wondered why anyone would want to hear my story. After all, *it is just my life,* I reasoned. For me, it was another devastating loss tacked on to a string of losses and disappointments that were already mine, and all I wanted to do was get in a corner and make the world go away. What I found, however, is a sense that many people who had not experienced that same kind of loss could relate to me. It became clear to me that "Katrinas" can come in many forms. My loss was mine, and theirs was theirs, but the process of finding peace and healing following any kind of loss is a journey for all, no matter our race, tax statuses, educational backgrounds, professions, or anything else. Despite my trepidation, I had encountered a door of opportunity to use my trial as a vehicle to reach out to others.

I've always believed that my gifts would make room for me. Yours will, too. What I mean by this is, whatever your contribution is to the world, i.e. your community, there are people waiting for you. Your paths will cross sooner or later. Can you imagine how unchanged the lives of many sick individuals would be if Dr. Robert Jarvik had not made his contribution to the medical community? Dr. Jarvik is known the world over as the inventor of the first permanent total artificial heart that has been beneficial to so many. The medical community was ready to receive the "gift" Dr. Jarvik shared with the world; his medical genius.

Think about Dr. Martin Luther King, Jr. Can you imagine a world without the contributions he made? His giftedness made room for him, because there was a great need, and he chose to meet it. His willingness to walk through that door of opportunity to move the world forward in civic and race relations has benefited all of us. Now consider the thousands of people who donate their time mentoring young people or tutoring them in academic subjects. Consider also the many volunteers

A Window of Time and a Door of Opportunity

across this nation and the world who commit their lives to serving others in numerous ways. Their "gifts" have made room for them and they are meeting needs!

This principle is a biblical concept; it is not some famous person's quote. ***"A man's gift maketh room for him, and bringeth him before great men."*** (Proverbs 18:16, KJV). My greatest desire is to use the spiritual gifts that God has given me to positively affect as many people as possible. I don't worry about who will read my books or who will come to hear me speak. What I *do* believe is that this message of hope will find its way to those who are ripe and ready to receive it. Our paths have not crossed by chance, but rather by divine purpose. It isn't about me at all, actually. It is simply my determination to help people who are hurting. I'm not going to sit around and wait until all of my problems are solved. No, my healing comes as I give and as I share and put forth every effort to encourage others.

I believe in living an authentic life with no room for make-believe. This means that, while you're reaching out to others, you have no need to pretend that you have yourself totally together. Perhaps you're still seeing a licensed therapist or spiritual counselor, so continue if that helps you. Maybe you're taking anti-depressants or having to keep a journal to help promote your own inner healing. That is perfectly okay! Remember, there is no reason to feel any shame. Most of the people you know are dealing with major challenges, and guess what? They're confused and scared out of their wits, too. B.C. Forbes said, "You have no idea how big the other fellow's troubles are." I believe that life exempts no one.

When I was writing the business plan for L.I.F.E.Talk Communications, my speaking and writing venture, I came to the part where I had to decide who my target audience would be. In other words, I had to know who I could best serve. I suddenly realized that because my work focuses on encouraging and inspiring people, it was safe to say that it would put the average person in my target group. Now, it may be that some people are too prideful to *admit* that deep down inside they're hurting but that doesn't change the fact that they are.

It's very easy to recognize people who *look* the part of having it all together, whether they're in our churches, our social circles, or in

45

Between: Getting From Where You Are To Where You Want To Be

the marketplace. But things are not always as they appear, right? It's amazing what a little makeup, a fresh haircut, a face lift, or a designer wardrobe can do to make someone look like he or she has arrived and has conquered all of his or her fears and insecurities. If you think you're the only person struggling with fears and insecurities, think again. I've learned that it's sometimes the person who is wheeling the most authority that's the most insecure and fearful. They, too, have made huge mistakes in life, so we're in the 99th percentile. The other one percent, who haven't made any blunders, have probably already been translated into heaven!

Now, back to you; would you at least do yourself one favor? Would you make a promise to, at the minimum, stay open to the possibility that one day you *will* come through the frustration of your many losses, setbacks, disappointments, and personal mistakes? Allow your mind to travel past those things and see yourself being of service to others. Is there a childhood pastime or goal you can fall back on? Is there a lifelong passion buried deep down inside of you? Perhaps it's time to unearth that passion again.

I've encountered both men and women who are looking for purpose in their lives. Perhaps they've enjoyed prosperous careers or traveled the world or attained certain goals, but they still find themselves living without purpose or without having made genuine contributions to the betterment of humanity. Living a life marked with purpose takes deliberate action. You don't just wake up one morning and receive your life's purpose from the sky. Pay attention to your life. I believe one's purpose will manifest when their window of time for healing intersects with their door of opportunity to reach out and serve others.

Let's start with something simple. Are you a good swimmer? Maybe you can volunteer at your local YMCA to teach other adults how to swim. And let me know when you decide to do that. I would sign up to be your first recruit! Or consider the many senior citizens who suffer from loneliness and often don't eat well simply because they don't have anyone to enjoy meals with. I've known elderly people who've actually had meals from the *Meals on Wheels* organization left at their doorsteps, but who didn't eat the food because they had no one to

46

A Window of Time and a Door of Opportunity

sit with them. You could volunteer to go to have lunch with a senior citizen once or twice a week. Trust me; elderly people have experienced so much, that their life stories will certainly encourage you to make it through your challenges. They will make you laugh, too! And laughter has been proven to be as effective as any good medicine. My maternal grandmother lived to the young age of 102, and the stories she told were incredible. Her sense of humor would help anyone to get a balanced perspective on their life.

> *We are all faced with a series of great opportunities brilliantly disguised as impossible situations.*
> *– Chuck Swindoll*

What is your restless desire? I'm not advocating that if a person gets involved with community service or ministry that he or she will be cured of all emotional and psychological ailments; not at all. What I am saying is that it's a vehicle that can help you to feel valued when low self-esteem and lack of confidence may be taking you down like a ferocious pit bull. More importantly, at the same time, someone else's needs are being met through you. As Chuck Swindoll, my favorite bible study teacher, once said, "We are all faced with a series of great opportunities brilliantly disguised as impossible situations."

Chapter Recap

- Take as much time as you need to heal, but when you're at your lowest point and think that you've got nothing to give, you might actually be in the best position to do so.
- Turn your most pressing pain into the perfect pain, by using it as a catalyst to reach out to help others, and yourself.
- You don't have to wait until you've solved all your own problems before you can be a blessing to someone else.
- Start with something simple.

Between: Getting From Where You Are To Where You Want To Be

Questions and Thoughts to Ponder

1. Describe a life experience in which you needed a window of time for healing.
2. Have you ever sensed that your "door of opportunity" was right across the way from your "window of time"? What helped you to realize that? Talk or write about it.
3. Have you ever participated in any kind of volunteer work? How did it make you feel?
4. How do you think your contribution made the benefactors of your volunteer service feel?

Dare To Do This

Search online for non-profits whose focus speaks to you. Contact them about volunteering. Check with your church or synagogue as well, because churches and synagogues often partner with non-profit organizations who serve their nearby communities or even distant communities.

Chapter Eight

Keepers

> *We sometimes too easily rid ourselves of people, things, and situations that may prove to be extremely valuable to us down the road. We shouldn't be so anxious to shake ourselves loose of everything that makes us feel uncomfortable. We first need to make sure they're not "keepers!"*

I remember the day my niece Nichole met my fiancé. She said, "Girl, where did you meet *him*? "He's a keeper!" I cracked up with laughter at that, but more so at the way she said it. Encarta's World English Dictionary defines a keeper as *something that is worth keeping, especially a fish that is large enough to be legally caught and retained*. Well, I know very little about fishing, but I'm glad that O'Donovan got caught up in my net because he is definitely worth retaining!

I recently took some things out of storage. In the process, my teenage daughter said to me, "Mother no! Don't throw that away! I need to keep some things from my childhood!" I think we finally decided to keep one of her baby blankets, her *Easy Bake* oven, and an art table and chair. Having limited space in her room, we weren't sure where we would put those things, but to my daughter, they were sure keepers! Things can easily accumulate where we need it least – our homes,

49

Between: Getting From Where You Are To Where You Want To Be

minds, and hearts – but it's important to periodically clean those spaces out even though it means struggling to decide what to keep and what to throw away.

I have the tendency to be a pack rat, so perhaps my daughter inherited that horrible habit from me. You've met my type. I believe everyone has at least one of us in his or her life. Somehow, I've convinced myself that *everything* is worth keeping. I've kept just about every school project, test, and writing assignment that the children have ever done. I also hang on to clothes I can no longer fit into, in hopes that I'll get back down to a size 8 by the time they come back in style. And, of course, I keep all of those blessed Wal-Mart receipts!"

I do have some regrets, though. After I moved back into our family home in New Orleans, following our father's death and my devastating divorce, I was in such a mental fog and state of depression that I cleaned out the house and threw away hundreds of old 45 records. What was I thinking!? I remember all of those old Motown hits of the 60's and 70's, and hearing the "record man" coming down the street blasting the latest hits from a giant speaker mounted to the top of his van. I can *still* hear myself screaming, "Momma, the record man is coming!" Momma loved herself some Al Green! I loved the Jackson 5. Let's not talk about Smokey Robinson & the Miracles, Stevie Wonder, The Stylistics, Marvin Gaye, and The Supremes! With eleven brothers and sisters, the 45 hits kept rolling into our home. Darn it! They were keepers! And I threw them all away.

Mental funks can cause us to do things like that. Sometimes we throw away good relationships, with good people, simply because we can't get ourselves together. And often the other person is willing to wait for us and help us along our journey. We have to learn to trust again. Maybe at times we just experience episodes of emotional meltdowns or something. Even the IRS tells us that we should hold on to our records for at least *three* years! Yet we sometimes too easily rid ourselves of people, things, and situations that may prove to be extremely valuable to us down the road. We shouldn't be so anxious to shake ourselves loose of everything that makes us feel uncomfortable, without first making sure they're not "keepers."

Keepers

Most of us travel, and when we do, we usually feel the need to go shopping for souvenirs. Shopkeepers depend on us to purchase little trinkets that will remind us and our loved ones of where we've been. When my husband and I were on our honeymoon, we certainly bought our share of little tokens. But why do we need those little tangible reminders? Being human, we like to feel things. We like to hold and see stuff in our hands. But what about those things that are not so tangible yet are ever so valuable? What about the promises we make to ourselves, to our children, and to God? How come we sometimes so easily discard them?

You may be between some hard things right now, but I'm asking you to make a few promises to yourself. But you have to *keep* them. Make a promise to stop putting yourself down. And promise that you won't give up on life even when it feels like life has given up on you. We should all strive harder to be better promise keepers.

Have you ever heard the expression, "Don't throw the baby out with the bath water"? Well, some of you have thrown out your dreams, talents, and opportunities, just because you've suffered through some difficult things. Stop doing that. Hold on to your dreams, visions, goals, and aspirations! They're keepers!

Maybe you've been so frustrated with life that you deliberately tossed out your best "possessions". Well shucks, by all means, go rummaging through the back alleys, trash cans, and drain pipes of life and recover them! Your dreams and aspirations will serve as your best motivators while you recover from the mental, financial, or professional slumps you presently find yourself in. Not long ago, I lost my key ring with all of my keys on it. It took me two days to go through everything in my home. My biggest fear was someone finding my keys and getting access to my family, car, and home. I needed to find my keys before anyone else found them. And for some strange reason, after I found myself out of options, it occurred to me that I needed to check the kitchen trash can. Yep, you guessed right. My entire set of keys was in there! I felt as though I had been reunited with a bunch of long lost friends!

Perhaps you've *inadvertently* thrown away the "keys" to the way out of your current dilemma. Just think of the doors you would gain access to if you find your keys! Now, go back and find them because they're the keys of life. They're keepers! I often think of how my lost keys opened doors to some very important things. I really needed to find those keys!

What about you? What keys have you lost? You don't want anyone else to find your missing keys because that person might exploit you. They might open some of your "doors" and steal your greatest opportunities. And you cannot afford to let that happen.

> *If for some reason you've already tossed out your best possessions, well shucks, by all means go rummaging through the back alleys, trash cans, and drain pipes of life and recover them! Your dreams, visions, and aspirations will serve as your best motivators while you recover from the mental, financial, or professional slumps you presently find yourself in.*

Here are some important "keeper keys" for living. Familiarize yourself with them. If you are missing any of these, go after them with all of your heart and soul!

1. **Key of Faith** – Faith is the real meat of everything you're hoping for. Have faith in God!
2. **Key of Self-Encouragement** – It's the positive *self-talk* that will make the difference for you. Don't depend on others to make you feel valuable.
3. **Key of Hope** – When we lose hope, we're most apt to give up on ourselves. Never embrace giving up as an option.
4. **Key of Integrity** – Without this key, life continues down a very deceptive path. Trust yourself and give others reasons to trust you.
5. **Key of Enthusiasm** – Become a cheering squad of one! Stay excited about your future, even though your present situation may look grim.
6. **Key of Optimism** – Try to see the positive in everything.

Keepers

7. **Key of Laughter** – Laughter really is good medicine for your soul. Find something to laugh at!
8. **Key of Persistence** - The race is not won by the swift, but by the one who endures to the end.
9. **Key of Patience**- Be patient with yourself!
10. **Key of Appreciation** - Learn to appreciate all of life's experiences, even the bad ones. They help to shape you into the person you need to become.

Chapter Recap

- Sometimes we inadvertently throw away things that we should keep, especially when we're mentally tired.
- Wait awhile. Then take time to sift through some things (relationships, ideas, etc.) to make sure, before tossing them out.
- Hold on to your dreams, visions, goals, and aspirations. They're keepers!
- Learn about life's important "keeper" keys.

Questions and Thoughts to Ponder

1. Is there something in your life that was worth keeping, but that you instead discarded?
2. Revisit my list of "keeper keys" above. What important life keys do you feel are slipping away from you right now?
3. Which life keys have you already lost?
4. Which of the "keeper keys" would be most important for you to have at this stage in your life? For instance, do you need more hope? More enthusiasm? More integrity?

Dare To Do This

Go back and retrieve something in your life that you threw away, whether it was a dream, a relationship, or your enthusiasm for living.

53

Chapter Nine

The Appearance of Things

> *Honesty is the first chapter of the book of wisdom.*
> *- Thomas Jefferson*

We've all heard it before. Things may not be as they appear. The cosmetic industry is a thriving, multi-billion dollar operation that is driven by consumers concerned with their appearance. For some, a routine makeover is not enough and they're somehow convinced that they're in need of extreme makeovers. Many invest in face lifts, cosmetic dental work, and extensive surgical procedures to change how they look.

Realistically, though, appearances go much deeper than cosmetics. Many are stuck between how their life appears to the outside world and how it is in reality. What about you? Perhaps you've succeeded in impressing people from the outside, but inside, you're a wreck, and you feel diminished and powerless. You have to make up your mind about where you are on this issue because you won't be able to live between two appearances for very long. It can wear you out! An appearance is sometimes merely a performance in front of a public audience. It's only an attractive but very shallow kind of thing; a veneer which often accomplishes the goal of hiding the real thing. Your audience might be your colleagues at work or your social club members. They might be your circle of friends, church family, neighbors, or even your personal family; all who may have specific impressions or expectations of you. Have you faked them all out?

There's something about that public thing, though. It's so easy to appear that we have it all together in public. It's like seeking to create particular impressions to others, but once we put it out there, we have to keep those appearances up, and that might feel like running on a treadmill that never stops! That is not what we want. I believe we should strive just as hard to make positive impressions in our personal lives, to ourselves, away from the lights, camera, and all of the action.

> *It's easy to appear that we have it all together in public.*

Life can do a flip-flop really fast on us. Usually, we don't see ahead of time that life changes are on the horizon for us. Changes can be provoked by *any* of the many issues of life, at any moment, and in the twinkling of an eye. For the longest time, your life may have appeared to be on track, but maybe you've been caught off guard. Right now, you may be thinking that you went to the right schools and studied the right curriculum; married the right person, who has the right career; moved into the right house, in the right neighborhood; joined the right church or synagogue, *and* placed your membership with the right social club. Now you're 30, 40, or 50-something, and you're no longer impressed with your alumnus status, your gated community, your social club membership, or your career. That's forcing you to redefine what it means to have made all the "right" choices.

If, by chance, you're not happy with the way your life is right now, know that you can make some productive changes. You're probably aware that something is missing, and you *do* want to do something about it. Could it be that for most of your adult life you've been consumed with "the appearance of things?" If so, then you're most likely tired of trying to keep up those appearances (which can be mentally and physically

Between: Getting From Where You Are To Where You Want To Be

exhausting), and you're ready to take on a lifestyle of more authentic living. The time to do that is now.

We're living in a time when people are losing their homes and their livelihood in record numbers, so time has run out for fake living. Be certain of this: material things can *disappear* a lot quicker than they appeared in our lives, so we can't place our hope in *things*. That kind of hope floats. We need to let God be our anchor of hope. I'm reminded of a song we used to sing a lot at my home church. The lyrics were, "my hope is built on nothing less, than Jesus blood and righteousness". If you haven't already, I'd really encourage you to rethink your life in the light of a personal relationship with the Lord Jesus Christ. I know you might not be open to my suggestion, but I believe that real living can only stem from a truly divine relationship with God. Others of you may have begun such a journey, but perhaps you might consider drawing even closer to Him. The spiritual and moral fabric of our world is unraveling more quickly than many would care to acknowledge. But life just has a way of forcing us to look at truth. And for you, this might be the perfect time to review some things.

You may not know how to begin such a journey towards more authentic or spiritually sensitive living, but the important thing is to start from where you are now. Then continue until you get to the place that gives you the peace you've been longing for. The Lord has promised to give you peace, and that is in his divine plan for your life. (See John 14:27) Seek him!

Though your life may look picture perfect to an outside, envious world, you may be ready to break free from the pretense of it all. You may never know how many people you can help just by stepping outside of your situation. Maybe there are other people in your circle that feel they, too, are living unfulfilled lives, but they're terrified to admit that to themselves or to their loved ones. Perhaps, like you, they too keep themselves busy with more and more *things*. They try to bury their feelings and continue to exist outside of their comfort zones. What could possibly be more uncomfortable than living a lie day after day after day? You may very well be the person to inspire others once you take your own initial step towards more authentic living.

56

The Appearance of Things

Honesty is always the first, and most painful, step. But it is definitely the best step! It may feel like you're performing open-heart surgery on yourself without any anesthesia. (Ouch!) But you have to stop pretending. Take off the mask, and look at yourself in a mirror – an actual mirror. Look deeply. Who and what do you really see? Be willing to come to grips with the naked truth, and then face it head on. I caution you that it will take some time to sift through some stuff, so don't be unreasonably hard on yourself. Allow God to give you an authentic identity. Let go of the fake one. You can trust God, because His intent is always to elevate you to a new level of conscious living that will not only honor Him but bless you at the same time.

You will need a lot of courage to embark upon this journey, but courage will replenish itself with each step you take. Inner peace and contentment is what you're after, and until you get real with balancing what your life *appears* to be like to others and what it actually is, peace will always elude you. Your decision to live more authentically might confuse and upset those who have been in your inner circle for years. But don't take responsibility for anyone's reaction. And don't beat up on yourself about anything. Take your time, and do an accurate assessment of where you are in life so you can set valid and reachable goals to get to where you know you need to be.

When you're hurting, it may seem like the only thing you have to hold on to, is the appearance of things. What a wonderful time to do some deep soul searching. Have you been kidding yourself all of these years? Only you know the answer to that question. If you take away the mansion, the fancy cars, the bulging bank accounts, the position of power, and the social status, what are you left with? You see, when you remove all appearances, you just might have to get to know your real self. Do you really know yourself? Taking the time to really get to know yourself can be scary, but don't worry. Your life has given you permission to freely explore your own heart. Access granted. Go there!

It's never too late in fiction or in life to revise.
– Nancy Thayer

57

Between: Getting From Where You Are To Where You Want To Be

Now, the door of opportunity is opened to you to do something about your situation. If you would but peek through that door, you will almost immediately sense the reality of your great worth and value, and that's vital, especially if you've ever been told that you aren't worth much. Perhaps you've come to understand that hiding behind appearances only causes internal suffering. God bless you! You're on your way to true healing and real liberation. The need to hide behind the appearance of things will no longer exist because your quest for more authentic living will validate you more than any padded bank account, luxury car, or prestigious career could ever do. But you didn't know any of these things before this point, so don't sweat about it. It's all a part of your unique journey on the road to realizing your true purpose for being here.

The idea is to have your outer appearances substantiated by genuine living that is motivated by sincerity and integrity. No more fluff! You've entered into a different phase; this is where you want to make some real changes in your life. Heraclitis said, "It is in changing that things find purpose." You are *between*. I challenge you right now to start re-evaluating every one of your preconceived notions about what makes for a fulfilled life.

> *The need to hide behind the appearance of things will no longer exist because your quest for more authentic living will validate you more than any padded bank account, luxury car, or prestigious career could ever do.*

On the other hand, you might be in that certain percentile of individuals who are thinking that you did not go to the right schools, take the right course of studies, marry the right person, make the right professional decisions, or involve yourself with the right social groups. You're on the opposite side the spectrum. Well, there's news for you, too! You're in my group. Sometimes things may appear to be over for you, but this is not necessarily so. All of those seemingly wrong choices

58

The Appearance of Things

still helped to prepare you for what is ahead in your future. There's a divine purpose in everything. Your cake is not baked yet, and your casserole is still in the oven. There are still some things that you can do to turn your life around for the better. Life is all about choices, and as long as you have breath, you can affect your life by the choices you make. I am urging you to make the choice to go on, regardless of your situation.

If you thought that last setback would take you down for the last time, it hasn't; and it won't. You can still make the choice to go forward, and live out your newly discovered life-purpose. Just imagine someone out there longing to hear your story of perseverance. It doesn't matter that you're still going through challenges. You're still here, and there's a lot to be said for that. Imagine someone on the brink of despair, praying for a ray of light to penetrate their darkness. Yes, that ray of light and hope could possibly be you. Let God use you! Don't wait until you stop hemorrhaging. You can't afford to wait that long; you have things to do. That person who needs your touch, your story, and your energy, cannot wait that long. You are highly valuable to your family, yourself, and to your community, even if you don't feel that you are. If you have to, then become a committee of one and cheer yourself on in spite of everything you're feeling.

Perhaps you think you've messed up so much that it's too late for you to make a positive contribution in life. Well, here's my question to you: Who determines the timing of things? Our times are in God's hands. I would like to make you aware of the possibility that this season of your life may be the perfect time for you to pull together all of your resources and start making things happen for you. Don't worry about how things in your life appear. Sometimes appearances lie to us! So, neither the good nor the bad appearances can be trusted. All of those setbacks were in the plan all along. I've had so many personal setbacks in my life that I've often wondered how they could possibly factor into the larger plan for my life. My faith, however, tells me that if I keep making positive deposits and healthy decisions in my life on a daily basis, then I will be victorious. It's not about the swiftness of things but rather about being persistent and enduring to the end.

Between: Getting From Where You Are To Where You Want To Be

Good things will find their way to you, and you will make a huge difference not only in your own life but in the lives of others. Don't be hard on yourself for any poor life choices you've made. Remember that things are not always as they appear, and you still have so much to give and to do. Like me, you may be a late bloomer. Maybe you're just discovering or just stepping into your true life-purpose. That, too, is okay. Believe in a brighter future for yourself! And keep in mind that it is *never* too late to embrace your authentic self.

> *You will need a lot of courage to embark upon this journey, but courage will replenish itself as you take one step at a time.*

Chapter Recap

- Many are stuck between how their life appears to the outside world and how it is in reality.
- Inner peace and contentment is what you're after, and until you get real with balancing what your life appears to be to others, and what it actually is, peace will always elude you.
- Don't be hard on yourself for any poor life choices you've made, because things aren't always as they appear. Your life is not over. You still have so much on the inside of you!

Questions and Thoughts to Ponder

1. Have outer appearances always been important to you? In what areas would that apply in your situation?
2. Are you a people pleaser? How, if at all, might you approach life differently?
3. Your life may *appear* to be beyond repair. How would your thinking change if you knew that was a lie?

The Appearance of Things

Dare To Do This

Get in front of an actual mirror. Look at yourself *and* your life through spiritual eyes. Take note of how your life *appears*. Then ask God to show you what you need to do to align your life with His plans and purposes for you.

Chapter Ten

Do You Know What You Really Want To Do?

> *"Try not to become a man of success but rather try to become a man of value"* – *Albert Einstein*

At some time in your life, you may have felt as though you were displaced, like you missed a beat, stood in the wrong line, or signed up for the wrong plan. Most people can relate to that feeling. But can you imagine what it would feel like to be doing something that reflects who you really are on the inside? It always amazes me how usually within a few minutes of making a new acquaintance we're inevitably asked, *"What do you do?"* Doesn't it feel great to be able to say, "I'm the CEO of such and such, or I'm the Director of such and such?" At least, that's probably what you've been trying to convince yourself of. But you and I know better. What you're really thinking deep down inside is that you wish you could say you're living your God-inspired dream, and following your passion.

I know so many people who spend countless hours, and even years, doing something other than what they'd rather be doing or investing huge sums of money, time and effort pursuing things they don't really want. Believe me, it takes guts to follow your heart, but sometimes that is the only way to experience peace and fulfillment. Wouldn't it be great if you could merge what you're doing now with who you really are? In

62

Do You Know What You Really Want To Do?

that way, you would be empowered to live more authentically. Let's say, for instance, that you've always dreamed of owning and operating a gourmet bakery, and you decide once and for all to pursue it. First, you'll need to come out of hiding and stop living in pretense. And that is not always easy to do. Then you'll need to pull every resource you have to make that happen for you.

If you've allowed your current title or position to define you when in fact it's misrepresenting who you really are, it might be time to reconsider some things. And what would you do if you lose your current title or position? That's something to think about too. It may be that you're afraid of what others may think if you say, "*Though I do this or that, I have really been feeling so out of place, and out of tune with who I am on the inside. I think I'm going to take the plunge and do something or build a career that speaks to who I really am.*"

It may be that it is *you* who is really standing between what you're actually doing now and what you really want to do. Have you identified what your true passions are, or where you want to be in the various areas of your life in the future? It could be that at this juncture of your life all you know is that you need to move from the place where you are, though it need not be a physical move. In reality, this could apply to almost any area of your life. Then again, you might need or want to make a geographical move. Sometimes our blessing is literally in another physical place.

Maybe you need to move away from family and close associations in order to reach your destiny. God told Abraham that in order to seize his best opportunity he had to move away from what was familiar to him. **"Leave your country, your people, and your father's household, and go to the land I will show you. I will make you into a great nation, and I will bless you; I will make your name great, and you will be a blessing."** (Genesis 12:1-2). Sometimes things that are familiar to us cause us to cling to our current situation much longer than we need to, and hinder us from embracing new possibilities for our lives. So, perhaps you *should* consider leaving those familiar things in order to step into your destiny, whatever that is for you.

On the other hand, if you're a person who has been away from your family or hometown for ten, twenty, or even thirty years or more, the

Between: Getting From Where You Are To Where You Want To Be

time may have come for you to go back there. Maybe your season is up at the place where you've been living these many years. Sometimes, moving back home (even temporarily) can help us regain composure after life has knocked us down. It helped me to do just that after my divorce. It might not be an easy move, but hopefully you will see the blessing in it, as a possibility. Now, if you've strayed away spiritually, then you will definitely want to "go back home". Ask God to take you back, spiritually speaking, to the place where you first believed in Him.

Sometimes things that are familiar to us cause us to cling to our current situation much longer than we need to, and hinder us from embracing new possibilities for our lives.

What do you really want to do? Do you want to improve your health? How are you going to get to a place of physical health and vitality when you're experiencing a downward spiral in your condition? First, you must imagine yourself being healed and know that you are deserving of healing. Then do what you can do to improve your physical health. Do you really want to be made whole? What about your finances? Are you broke? Have you become comfortable with living from paycheck to paycheck? You know you deserve better. You know you should be the lender and not the borrower, but it can be so scary to take a different path. Where would you like to be in your life? You just might have to get out of your own way.

So many people that I talk to are not happy with some area of their lives, but they lack the passion, drive, and/or vision to see beyond where they are now. They feel stuck. They are *between*. But I believe that there are unlimited resources at their disposals. All of heaven will be summoned to their side if they would only begin to drive the roots of their dreams deeper and deeper into their realities through daily pursuits.

As for you, don't *you* settle! You cannot choose that option if you want to make progress. Maybe you are experiencing what was supposed

64

Do You Know What You Really Want To Do?

to be the "job of your dreams" or your "dream life", but deep down, you're feeling very displaced. What are you going to do about it? There is something so powerful about listening to yourself and being true to who you are.

> *What is your passion? Passion will drive you into your destiny faster than anything else can.*

Allow me to tell you a true story. In the mid-eighties, I worked as a dental hygienist in a private office. I remember one particular patient who impressed me with how he went after what made him happy. He was a well-educated man and a mechanical engineer with a private firm. I remember how I used to compliment him on the beautiful pull-over sweaters he wore. One day, he told me that as a child, his grandmother had taught him how to knit. He went on to say that he'd always had a deep passion for knitting and finally decided to pursue it. He began by knitting and wearing his own sweaters because it made him feel so good. Plus, it was free advertising!

Soon afterwards, he began receiving many requests for sweaters from friends and colleagues who admired his work. Eventually, he decided to quit his successful job as an engineer and start his own knitting business! His sweaters became so in-demand that he began teaching knitting classes in order to hire qualified people to help him with the rapid growth of his business. I remember how happy he was, after previously feeling so out of place with his career in engineering, and finally making the decision to pursue his real passion.

So what are your skills and gifts? Maybe you don't even think of your skills or hobbies as gifts. But that may be the very bridge to get you from where you are now to where you want to be. For me, I've always felt blessed with the gift of communication and connecting with people. So I thought, *why not get paid for something I've been doing for thirty years without pay?* When your aspirations are God-inspired, it's as if miracles happen to help you get the task accomplished. The right people will come into your life and the right circumstances will move in your favor. Think about it.

Do you aspire to use your skills to serve others? There are billions of people in the world, so you can't possibly run out of people to be a blessing to. If this worldly vision is too large for you, then you might want to consider the number of people in your city, or town, or your neighborhood. Sometimes, people don't even realize what their needs are until they're presented with the services you're willing to provide. It'll be as if you've jogged not only their thinking but their very souls. One way to think of it is to consider what you would be willing to commit your life to doing even if you couldn't get paid for it. Can you imagine doing what you love to do while at the same time bringing joy to others by making positive differences in their lives?

My brother, Wayne, has a true passion to positively affect the lives of young people by coaching them in track and field. He coaches both on the track and in the "field" of life. He allows nothing and no one to move him away from that endeavor. At the end of his workday as an Information Technology Specialist, and often on the weekends, he shifts into doing what really drives him on the inside, positively impacting the lives of young people. And often, many of the young men and women he coaches have no father in their lives. Of course, his regular job provides a comfortable living for him, but coaching is his passion. And though he doesn't receive monetary pay for using his skills as a track coach, I'm sure he can testify to the "rewards" he's received over the years.

> When you cease to make a contribution, you begin to die" – Eleanor Roosevelt

Are you facing an inner conflict because you're not living up to your full potential? What I'm talking about has absolutely nothing to do with how successful you are in your career, where you live, what kind of car you drive, or whether you're wealthy in stocks. Isn't there more to life than amassing a lot of *things* and comforts for ourselves and our loved ones? Is there anything that you're doing to positively enhance

Do You Know What You Really Want To Do?

the life of another person? Is there some contribution that you would consider making, even if it might mean making some sacrifices on your end? Can you imagine what it would feel like to smile on the *inside*? That can only happen when you're living out your life's purpose, while at the same time, doing all you can to make a positive difference in the lives of others. Just think about it. The essence of life encompasses more than just getting up and going to work every day, even if your work is meaningful to you.

So, let me ask you this: does life consist of the abundance of *things* or of the abundance of moral convictions, values, and living to one's fullest potential? You be the judge. But please understand that I'm certainly not encouraging you to run into your office on Monday morning and hand in your resignation. *(Who would do that in this economy anyway, right?)* Stop, think, and pray. Your highest calling can certainly be lived out in addition to a regular nine to five. For many years, I did inspirational speaking for free, in both religious and secular events, while in college and while working fulltime jobs. In addition, I spent twelve years volunteering in various prisons, speaking to incarcerated men and women, and often reaching out to their family members as well. Seek your own guidance and wisdom on what is right for you. Just remember to be true to who you are.

> *"The service we render others is the rent we pay for our room on earth"* - *Sir Wilfred Grenfell*

Chapter Recap

- Many have felt professionally and spiritually displaced at some point.
- Consider that maybe the season for where you are living or what you have been doing is over.
- Many people cringe when asked, *"What do you do?"* This may be because they know their life's work is not reflecting who they really are, and what they really want to do.

Between: Getting From Where You Are To Where You Want To Be

- I believe that fulfilled living happens when you're living out your life's purpose while simultaneously doing all you can to make a difference in the lives of others.

Questions and Thoughts to Ponder

1. Do you think that people will laugh if you tell them what it is that you would like to do as your life's work (or in addition to what you're doing in your career)?
2. How can you inspire others (particularly young people) to pursue careers, that will provide more than just a "good job", but that will bring them fulfillment and allow them to positively impact the lives of others?

Dare To Do This

If you're very successful in your career but are feeling displaced, the next time someone asks you what you do, try to answer the question honestly without feeling unfaithful to the real you. You don't have to impress other people.

Chapter Eleven

Moving Forward

> *I couldn't wait for success, so I went ahead without it.*
> *— Jonathan Winters*

Do you think it's possible for a person to inadvertently prolong their *between* phase by their own inaction or faulty thinking? In other words, how hungry are you to see your own goals achieved? If I were to ask you if you want your goals achieved, inevitably you would utter a resounding "yes!" I'd told myself the same thing time and time again, but the more I thought about it, the more I had to ask myself some tough questions. *Why wasn't I moving forward with my dream to become a successful writer of inspirational books and improve upon my inspirational speaking career? What was I really afraid of? Did I not think that I deserved to succeed? Why was I allowing complacency and negative self-thoughts to hold me back?*

What about you? How much effort are you willing to put into the preparation needed to bring about the achievement of your goals? I often watch my 13-year old son bake cakes from scratch, and I'm impressed with the amount of time he spends just preparing the ingredients, meticulously measuring and mixing everything together before it goes into the pan and then into the oven. It's that kind of thorough

Between: Getting From Where You Are To Where You Want To Be

preparation that assures him of a perfect cake every time. Like my son, you should be practicing your skills or ideas meticulously. The time and effort you put into preparing yourself will play a vital part in helping you to achieve great things. Doors tend to fly open to us when we're prepared for opportunity.

Even if you're naturally good at what you do (like playing a musical instrument, for example), you should still put in regular and earnest practice. My brothers, John and Theron, are both professional musicians. And I've seen both of them practice their instruments relentlessly, and it has really paid off for them!

Would you like to start writing encouraging notes to the troops overseas? Then just start. Would you like to learn to knit blankets and booties for newborn babies of needy families? Maybe you can start by taking a class to learn how to knit or crochet. How about this one? Are you good at fixing things? Maybe you can repair broken bicycles to give to needy children. Start making preparations to do those things. Move forward!

Some time ago, I realized that even though I'd developed an outline for a seminar I wanted to teach, I had not actually put the content of the seminar together. I had succeeded only in putting together an impressive outline. I shuddered at the thought of what I would do if a prospective client actually invited me to present that particular seminar. I painfully imagined myself scrambling to write the seminar curriculum text while making it look as though I'd been working on it for a very long time. It then occurred to me that I'd been cheating myself. I'd gotten so comfortable with my ability to quickly and easily write speeches and articles that I assumed I could do the same for a seminar curriculum.

Writing and speaking usually comes very naturally for me. However, writing a seminar curriculum was a horse of a different color. It was at this point that I realized I didn't want to succeed as badly as I had deceived myself into thinking I did. This was a different ball game. Putting together an entire seminar was more challenging than writing a 30 to 45 minute keynote speech, during which my audience was basically subjected to my oratory skills for a predetermined length of time. With a seminar curriculum, I had to factor in audience participation and perhaps also time for people to do soul searching in the presence of others. I needed to be prepared with more than the mere rhetorical questions that my speeches generally afforded. I had to have pointed questions to be addressed in group settings. I couldn't run from the participants' questions and concerns. I needed to be truly girded up for the task.

> *I wanted to build a successful inspirational writing and speaking career, but I was actually stunting my own growth without realizing it.*

My commitment to succeed was beginning to take on a different characteristic. Time and prayer taught me that I was not as ready as I had previously thought I was to relocate to the next destination of my career. I was squeezed between my dream and its fulfillment. I knew that my audience was out there, but I was actually prolonging my frustrating *between* phase because I had not done all that I knew how to do to prepare for them. I knew they deserved better. I wanted to improve upon my inspirational writing and speaking career, but I was actually stunting my own growth without realizing it. Now, I'm on a different kind of mission because I know that the fulfillment of a dream cannot come to an unprepared person.

Whatever your contributions are, your benefactors will find you when you're ready to present yourself to them. Is it a song, a book, a business, a ministry idea, a consumer product, an idea to benefit your neighborhood, or an idea for a medical cure? Often, by our own apathy, we make the world wait on us longer than they should have to. Our gifts, skills, and ideas must be honed and prepped for a waiting world. We have the supply. The demand is out there. But the two have not crossed paths yet, and this is perhaps for a valid reason. I'm not saying that we have to reach a point of perfection first, but that we should be prepared to face the challenges of starting out from where we are now.

> *"I will study and prepare myself, and then someday my chance will come." – Abe Lincoln*

When planning out my seminar, I didn't have a full appointment book of speaking engagements, and initially that concerned me. I also had neither editor nor publisher for my book. What I *did* possess was the desire to see others uplifted, and the drive to use my gifts and talents for the purpose I believed God had given them to me. That proved to be enough to serve as a springboard for me to further press my way to achieving my goals.

Soon, I began to sense an uneasiness that was not going to go away until I saw my dreams come to fruition. I stepped up my game. Then I thought about a quote I'd read by comedian Jonathan Winters: "I couldn't wait for success, so I went ahead without it". My prayers became more aggressive. I committed to resuming the writing of this book. Then I waited for my completed work to find its editor, its publisher, its audience, and so on because I knew that they would find me, too. It would surely happen, I told myself. I knew in my spirit that it was meant to be. As I moved forward, my vision assumed more definition. I sensed that the gap between where I was and where I wanted to be was closing. I called my future assistance team and my future audience into being by faith, and by completing my part of the dream, which was to complete my work first. What I had to share was the very best of myself, as is. And I made no apology for that.

All that I've just described can happen for you as well. Determine where you want to be, then make sure that you've done all you can humanly do to usher your dreams into reality. Your next step is to leave the rest to God's plan for your life. Live your life to the fullest, and live with expectation! And before you know it, you'll be experiencing the kind of fulfillment that I simply cannot find the words to express here.

Moving Forward

> *Everything you want is out there waiting for you to ask. Everything you want also wants you. But you have to take action to get it. - Jack Canfield*

Chapter Recap

- Don't wait for success. Go ahead without it!
- We have to do all that is humanly possible to reach our goals. Then leave the rest to God.
- Sometimes, because of our own apathy, we make the world wait for our contributions longer than it should have to.
- Live with expectation, to help usher in the most fulfilling life possible for you!

Questions and Thoughts to Ponder

1. Can you honestly say that you've done all you can humanly do to make your dreams come to pass?
2. In what ways have you possibly prolonged the interim phase between your goals and their achievement? In other words, do you have to get out of your own way?
3. Have you stopped pursuing your dreams because you were afraid that you didn't have the right connections?
4. Are you afraid of success?

Dare To Do This

Don't wait for anything or anybody. Write your vision down. Purchase whatever you might need to get started. Sign up for that class. Compose that song. Have your first interest meeting for the vision you have to turn your community around. Don't wait for success. Move forward!

Chapter Twelve

My Story, Your Story

> *I struggled through this manuscript because I was trying to write and encourage you without sharing my own story. That's when I got stuck. I just had to do what I've encouraged you to do; I had to face the shame.*

Don't be fooled by the title of this chapter. Initially, when I decided to focus on the topic of how to make positive choices in the midst of tough transitions, I struggled through the rough draft of this book. I actually created a problem by trying to write and encourage you without sharing my own story. That's when I got stuck. I just had to do what I've encouraged you to do; I had to face the shame. Eventually, it dawned on me that my story was actually embedded throughout the entire manuscript anyway; so I reasoned, that it didn't matter. Perhaps that's what makes for authentic writing. And though this account represents only a small part of my life story, I didn't even want to share the few personal nuggets you'll find written here, so I beg you to bear with me.

You see, in many ways I know you, and you know me, too, because our stories are not that different. Perhaps our circumstances are, but the stuff that makes for real life is all the same. Aren't you mulling

My Story, Your Story

over some things too? You, too, are reevaluating some things in your life. You, too, are trying to get a glimpse of what your life's purpose might be, after having experienced some devastating losses. Perhaps you live in an exclusively private community or near the shores of a beautiful ocean, while another reader might be living in the struggling neighborhoods of post-Katrina New Orleans. Maybe you're riding high on the crest of an illustrious career, while another reader just received a pink slip. Yet, there's a kindred thread that attaches us to one another, and this is it. In one way or another, we are all feeling *pressed between* where we are and where we want to be.

It's amazing how it's possible to be living out the same thing that you're writing about. What I mean is that I'm in the thick of having to move toward peace, healing, and victory in some areas of my own life as a result of a string of losses and life-altering mistakes. I've gone through a devastating divorce, lost two homes, and suffered from bouts of depression, anxiety, fear, and low self-esteem. I've also endured a house fire, job losses, the loss of a career, the loss of my parents, and the loss of two of my sisters. It's these kinds of losses, blunders and setbacks that make me not want to talk about me.

My teenage daughter thinks I should write an autobiography. But I don't think my life is that interesting. My daughter thinks otherwise. She's been watching me over the years. And she thinks it's "so cool" how I can stay encouraged even in the midst of loss, struggle, pain, and disappointment when those things are supposed to have beaten me down by now. She thinks that it's "cool" that I can be so encouraged that God still has many good things in store for my life. Here's the thing. I don't believe I can encourage you in something I haven't experienced myself. That's what I'm hoping this book will do, encourage and inspire you. You're hearing it from someone who has been there and in some ways is still "there."

I think I said it earlier, but just in case I didn't, I'll say it again: I am the queen of transitions! I know what it's like to have to start over, again and again. You develop a sense that stability eludes you. At times, I think that at my age I should be retiring from a career instead of working hard to establish another one. There are times I think that I should be on the back end of paying down a mortgage rather than

75

trying to put myself in a position to be able to purchase another home. I also think I should be in the position to be the lender and not the borrower, but that's not my current situation. Yet, my hopes are high, and I'm looking forward to things becoming even better than they've ever been in my life because not only am I working hard to ensure that, but my faith tells me so. Despite all of this, I'm convinced that I should be reaching out to others as I work through my own stuff. I'm an encourager by nature, so even if I'm in need of encouragement, I look for ways to lift up others first.

Life is full of changes. And it seems that the last sixteen years of my life have been decorated by a consistent string of them; some not so kind to me. I keep telling myself that God will use all of those setbacks and transitions to help me help others, and that somehow the reason behind them all will one day click and make sense to me. I ask God to allow me a life of stability, but when I think about it, I've had stability in many ways all along. Through trials and good times, my heart toward God has been the same, as has my love and nurturing ways toward my children. I still enjoy meeting and building relationships with people. I've tried to give of myself as much as possible to noble causes, and I still love to laugh! I'm healing with every key I press while writing this account, because it's reminding me that I'm still here. I'm still hopeful. I still have a lot to contribute. And it's *all* good.

> *I know what it's like to have to start over, again and again. You develop a sense that stability eludes you.*

I'm not so naive to think that my story is any more heart gripping than yours. I have sense enough to know that some of you have been through enough stuff to make my life look like a preschool fieldtrip to Fun-Land! That's why this is your story too! Some of you have experienced the death of your children. Others of you are battling chronic illnesses. Many of you are pressing through the pain of a loved

My Story, Your Story

one's addiction to drugs or alcohol. Some of you may have suffered the effects of terrible mistakes. Many of you have suffered the devastation of miscarriages. Sadly, many of you have been victims of some of the most horrendous acts of violence. Perhaps others have experienced sexual, physical or mental abuse as children, or even as adults. For many years, others of you have felt stuck between your dreams and your painful reality. But despite those things, our wide-ranging experiences have their own intrinsic value, hidden deep within the pain and hardship of it all.

For me, it seemed that over the past sixteen years, once I got through one crisis, another started. I moved back to my hometown following a devastating divorce, and started from scratch with my two young children. Then as soon as I felt myself being lifted, we suffered an electrical fire in the house our father built; the same house which gave me nothing but wonderful childhood memories. The same house I ran back to, to receive some much needed emotional healing after my divorce and my parents' deaths. With personal failures added to the mix of difficult losses, again, I was back at square one. I found another place for me and my children to live, and after a while, things started going well. I found a job I like, and resumed teaching at my church, where I met my current husband. Then, as fate would have it, Hurricane Katrina hit. Then I thought, *"Okay, God, and your point is?"*

I grew up in New Orleans, Louisiana, the eleventh of twelve children born to our parents, Charles and Rose Lewis. I remember having a wonderful upbringing with lots of people around me all the time. There was lots of music, laughter, and engaging conversations – always! We could not have had a better set of parents. I know all of my siblings would agree, and though we are all adults, our parents' deaths have left us stumbling in the dark, groping for the connection that existed before we lost them. I knew my parents were proud of me, their "baby girl," as my mother would often call me, and I lived and thrived on that. It made me want to be more successful in life. As an adult, though, as my life began to take several dark turns, I felt that I'd let my parents down. Now, I want nothing more but to make them, and my siblings, proud of me.

Between: Getting From Where You Are To Where You Want To Be

> *We could not have had a better set of parents. I know all of my siblings would agree, and though we are all adults, our parents' deaths have left us stumbling in the dark, groping for the connection that existed before we lost them.*

I loved my life growing up. I loved school and I had a lot of friends. We had a great neighborhood with wonderful families. But it was my parents and siblings who gave me the fondest memories of all. I enjoyed my journey all the way through high school and college, where I received a bachelor's degree in dental hygiene from Loyola University. When I started college, I thought I wanted to study civil engineering, but during my freshman year, I got interested in dental hygiene and switched my major. I remember that Dr. Robert McLean (who was one of my math professors and head of the Mathematics Department), tried to talk me out of making that change in my course of studies. He told me that with such a degree I would only be able to do "one thing", and that I would be stuck if I ever suffered from a disability that prevented me from practicing. But at eighteen years old and ready to conquer the world, I thought, *"What are you talking about? I'm young and healthy, and I can't imagine experiencing any kind of disability."* And I told him as much.

But Dr. McLean was speaking from experience. He had majored in chemistry and was permanently blinded when doing a chemical experiment, which is how he ended up teaching mathematics. Though I respected what he was telling me, I still didn't see how his point related to me. My thinking was that the world was going to have to open up and make room for me! What I had not thought about was the effects of many years (since the age of four), of relentlessly practicing my baton twirling in an effort to be like two of my older sisters. Like them, I had a goal to become a baton twirler when I got to high school, and I reached that goal and loved every minute of it.

My Story, Your Story

I did eventually get my license to practice dental hygiene, but after nine additional years of constantly twisting my wrists while practicing my profession, I was told that I'd caused a lot of damage to the tendons in both of my wrists. I began experiencing intense wrist pain while working with my patients, but my doctors erroneously attributed the pain to the hormonal changes in my pregnancy. (Isn't it funny how pregnancy gets a bad rap for a lot of conditions that ail women?) Actually, that had nothing to do with it. Later, a specialist diagnosed a condition called De Quervain's tenosynovitis, which is similar to Carpal Tunnel Syndrome. I had to come to grips with the reality that I was faced with a disability. It reminded me of Dr. McLean's admonition. That disability meant not only the loss of my career as a practicing dental hygienist, but my self-esteem took quite a hit as well.

Perhaps the goal of the divine Godhead was to give me as much strength training as possible through my long standing string of setbacks, disappointments, and trials. At least that's the way I try to reconcile things in my mind. And concerning that indelible day in August of 2005, many think that property was the main thing the families of the Gulf South lost during Katrina. But as important as that is, our losses go far beyond the material and the tangible. What we lost was the connection we enjoyed with family and friends.

During the hurricane's fury and aftermath, we were all dazed; in some ways, many still are. Since Katrina, we've struggled with confusion, post-traumatic stress, and the loss of our communities. Many were poor communities, but they were ours. Others were wealthier communities, but they were also ours. Many residents and evacuees still don't have the mental health services needed to help them to cope with the tragedy. Some have returned to live in their repaired homes or in FEMA trailers, but the essence of their neighborhoods is no longer there, and the truly depressing thing is, it probably won't ever be the same. At the time of this writing, our city is still struggling on every front, politically, spiritually, financially and socially; and it's turned into a criminal's oasis in some ways. It's going to take a while.

It's difficult to fully describe the devastating affect Hurricane Katrina has had upon my life. After the failure of my first marriage, I had returned to my native New Orleans with intentions to begin anew

79

Between: Getting From Where You Are To Where You Want To Be

and raise my children there, surrounded by the community that raised me. Many of the same families were still living in the neighborhood I grew up in, which helped me to feel a sense of wellness. Yet on that fateful Monday, from a Memphis hotel television, we watched along with the entire world, as Lake Ponchartrain emptied its massive self into our beloved city. The constant news coverage of the storm's aftermath and the breaking of the levees were numbing, as we all froze in disbelief. I had experienced many hurricanes in my lifetime, but I never imagined evacuating merely for fear of temporary inconveniences like no electricity and no water, only later to realize that we couldn't go back. It was the "big one" we in New Orleans had feared for so many years.

As I write this book, three years after the hurricane, we're still trying to cope and rebuild our city, our communities, and our lives. Unfortunately, many have survived Katrina's rage only to take their own lives. Some have moved on, while others have returned to what little they could salvage. It's hard for me to visit home now and witness the devastation that remains, especially in the Lower Ninth Ward. That place is in me, and I want to keep it there. It's where I learned my earliest life lessons, felt loved by family, and learned the real meaning of community. I'm glad my children had the chance to experience the Lower Ninth Ward, and call it home, before Katrina changed it forever. I am elated that they got the chance to share the same room that was once mine many years ago, and a chance to know some of the same people that positively impacted my life.

> *On that fateful Monday, from a Memphis hotel television, we watched along with the entire world, as Lake Ponchartrain emptied its massive self into our beloved city.*

From many of my past experiences, L.I.F.E.Talk Communications, my writing and speaking ministry, was born. But I was 18 years old when I first received, from God, the calling to use these gifts to uplift

My Story, Your Story

others. Recently, I began to sense a profound impression to use my writing skills in a more effective way; hence this book. I've always had a strong gift of connecting with people, and I've always loved to write. But until now, I had mostly used my teaching and speaking gifts through church ministries to speak at prisons, women's conferences, small group meetings, and such. My daddy taught me that it's important to speak and write well. He first noticed my writing skills when I entered an essay-writing contest at the age of fourteen. The essay I wrote was titled, "What I Would Give Back to My Community, If My Community Invests in Me." I won the contest. I still remember how impressed my father was with my writing! Prior to that, I hadn't thought much about my writing skills. Daddy bought me my own personal dictionary and thesaurus and told me to never stop writing. Not only was he an excellent writer himself, but his father, sister, and aunt were all published writers of their own books and articles. Additionally, in the 1940's his family published a monthly news magazine called "Twinkle". I still remember seeing that old typewriter and the old printing press still lying around when I was growing up. So, in some ways I feel compelled to write!

I'm constantly being asked how I can feel so comfortable speaking in front of so many people. It all started in elementary school when my teachers put me on stage quite often to speak at school assemblies. It's amazing how teachers can be so tuned in to the natural bents of their students. In fact, I even remember when I was in the 6th grade our principal had mercy on me one day, and decided to not suspend me from school as a result of being in a fight, simply because I was scheduled to speak the next day at a school function. Boy, did I feel relieved! (*To this day, I still don't know why my friend Janice decided to pick a fight with me. And it was over a ping-pong game during P.E. class!*) But at such a young age, it didn't occur to me that one day the gift of communication would manifest through a ministry of inspirational speaking and writing.

In the fall of 2005, I relocated to Virginia. With the hurricane still fresh in my broken heart, I was invited by a social worker to speak for a United Way-sponsored event as a hurricane Katrina survivor. I only agreed to do it out of a sense of commitment to give back to the local government and organizations that had reached out to the Katrina victims who had relocated to the Washington, D.C., metropolitan area, and around the country. Remember my essay about giving back to my community if they invested in me? I felt that I needed to make good on that promise. Still, I wanted that to be the end of it, because frankly, I was exhausted both physically and mentally from the challenges of life. But I guess God had other plans for me. I felt that my many setbacks had disqualified me from inspiring others, but I pressed on anyway.

At my children's prompting, I started a website in December of 2006. I solicited their help with the website, and when I told them I'd chosen "Lifetalk" as the name of my venture, my daughter suggested that I use the name as an acronym instead. From that, the name became "L.I.F.E.Talk Communications." We toyed with its meaning, but it soon occurred to me that the name should reflect my purpose and vision. My son came up with the idea of "living in faith." Hence, "L.I.F.E" stands for "Living in Faith with Expectation". The word "talk" simply represents the different mediums I hope to use to communicate to anyone needing inspiration and encouragement along life's journey.

You see, I'm a living example of the very thing I'm trying to encourage you to do. You may not be a writer or a speaker, but you can use what you've got. I guarantee you that the moment you decide to give back, more opportunities will find their way to you. For me, the joy I feel when I make a difference in someone else's life can sometimes make my own problems seem minuscule. Besides, this helps me to see purpose in my life story, which for many years I'd been confused about simply because I'd been pressed between so many things for such a long time. I want to encourage you to believe that your life story will take on its own definition and purpose as well, especially when you embrace your journey as uniquely yours.

Chapter Recap

- I struggled with this chapter because, honestly, I didn't want to tell my story.

My Story, Your Story

- Our stories aren't that different. Perhaps our circumstances are, but the stuff that makes for real life is all the same.
- I know what it is to have to start over again; many times.
- I believe that someday God will use the many transitions in my life for a greater good.
- He will use your life too.

Questions and Thoughts to Ponder

1. When you play back the videotapes of your life, what is it about *your* story that can definitely be used to encourage someone else?
2. None of us can go back and change anything about our lives, but in what ways do we have the power to write our own endings to our life stories?
3. I realize that my purpose is embedded in my life story. I think that yours is too.

Dare To Do This

If you haven't already done so, fully embrace the truth of your own life story, even the parts that you may think are neither useful to you nor to anyone else. You might be surprised how those past experiences will aid you in building a more promising future.

Chapter Thirteen

Biblical Characters Who Were Between Some Things

> *History merely repeats itself. It has all been done before. Nothing under the sun is truly new.*
> *- Ecclesiastes 1:12*

I love to study the lives of biblical personalities because it always reminds me that these individuals were in many ways just like you and me. Sometimes we tend to think that people in the Bible were so holy that they didn't experience real life as we know it. Well, nothing could be further from the truth! In fact, not only did these guys have to deal with many of the same life issues that we struggle with today, but often their trials were harsher because of the kind of societies in which they lived. In many ways we have been so spoiled and pampered by the conveniences of our modern society that we don't know how to endure difficult things without folding underneath the pressure of it all.

The wise man Solomon said, *"Nothing under the sun is truly new."* Many people in the Bible were *between* things and believe me; they endured a lot of messes in the middle of their journeys! Life happens to all of us, and it doesn't really matter what happens to us. What *does* matter is that we stay connected and allow our experiences to illuminate the way into brighter futures for us. Many biblical characters made mistakes, experienced frustration, depression, anxiety, discouragement,

84

loneliness, and suffered great losses, all of which is every bit a part of the human experience. But those who were wise came out victors because of *how* they dealt with it all.

> *I love to study the lives of people in the Bible because it always reminds me that these individuals were in many ways just like you and me.*

On the flip side, some biblical characters chose less beneficial ways of dealing with the *between* phases of their lives. They were too impatient to wait for the divine timing of things. For example, Abraham and his wife Sarah laughed at God's idea that one day they would bring forth the promised child, (Isaac), in their old age. Instead of trusting God's plan to move Sarah from barrenness to motherhood, they concocted a plan to get Sarah's handmaiden involved in their attempt to help God out. The result was that they ended up with Ishmael, who was not the child of promise. Theirs was an obvious lack of trust in God. They failed to see that God had an excellent plan to move them from emptiness to the kind of fulfillment that would last throughout many generations. Clearly, they wanted to skip the process, but it's the *process* that characterizes the *between* phases of our lives, and it's often where the meat of life's experiences are.

Saul was another one. He allowed dwindling resources and fear to cause him to go ahead of what the prophet Samuel had told him to do in battle. (I Samuel 13:6-13). He, too, was *between* some things; and he let pressure, impatience, and fear get the best of him. His decision to do this brought shame upon his kingdom, which was then taken away from him by God. You see, Saul was in constant fear of losing his position. We do ourselves a great disservice when we do things that cause us to forfeit the blessings God has for us, simply because we're holding on to a particular position (or a job or a career) for dear life. We've got to learn to just trust God on some things and handle our challenging *between* phases His way. Think about the CEO's and politicians in our current news stories that have been willing to do almost anything to hold on to their positions or statuses, only to later get caught and brought to public shame.

I've chosen to highlight, in more detail, the lives of five Old Testament biblical characters in an attempt to show that they handled the many uncomfortable interruptions in their lives with wisdom. These characters are Joseph, David, Ruth, Habakkuk, and Hannah. Joseph was between a dream and a prominent position in Egypt. David was between being anointed as Israel's next king and his eventual appointment to the throne. Ruth was between loss and redemption. Habakkuk was between a ruthless and violent society and the fulfillment of God's promise to put an end to it. And finally, Hannah was between barrenness and giving birth to one of Israel's greatest prophets.

I've dissected their stories to the best of my ability in order to support the premise of this book. But I want you to feel free to pick them apart as well. You might glean from their life stories the jewels I may have missed simply because I was at a different place than you when interpreting them. There is far too much wisdom here to exhaust. Put yourself in these individuals' places and feel their pain, their losses, their setbacks, their mistakes and their victories. Learn from their wisdom, their attitudes, their insights, and their obedience to God. These stories were written for our example, so let's extract from them all the ammunition we can muster to fight the good fight of faith which leads to triumph.

Their stories follow.

Chapter Fourteen

Habakkuk's Hardships

> *Has God ever told you to write some things down, and then wait for them to happen? Wait! So God, how long do you expect me to do that!?*

Do you have any hard questions for God? I know I have some. Still, I stand on the premise, and the promise, that "nothing is too hard" for Him. What makes our questions and concerns seem so difficult is the helplessness we feel when we are not in control of whatever our current situation happens to be. Often we're frustrated by our own human finiteness. And by the time we take our problems to God, we've likely already explored several ways to solve them; except God's way. Occasionally though, God will show us that we will just have to wait for some things to move in our favor. Has God ever told you to write some things down and then wait for them to happen? *Wait!? So God, how long do you expect me to do that!?*

Habakkuk went through this with the Lord. Evil was prevailing in his country, and he had some problems with God concerning it. He didn't understand how God, in all of His sovereignty, could seemingly sit back and allow evil to have full reign in the land. Habakkuk had some hard questions for Him. Not only is it perfectly normal to have

87

Between: Getting From Where You Are To Where You Want To Be

hard questions for God, but He really does want us to bring those questions and concerns to Him.

Listen to Habakkuk's cry: **"How long, O Lord, must I call for help? But you do not listen! Violence is everywhere! I cry, but you do not come to save. Must I forever see these evil deeds? Why must I watch all this misery? Wherever I look, I see destruction and violence. I am surrounded by people who love to argue and fight. The law has become paralyzed, and there is no justice in the courts. The wicked far outnumber the righteous, so that justice has become perverted."** (Habakkuk 1: 1-4). Sounds like our modern society, doesn't it?

What are your critical issues? You need answers, and you need peace. Have you lost your job? Did your home get swept away by the vicious floods of an unforgiving river? Do you have a chronically sick child? Have you received the heartbreaking news that the man who raised you is not your birth father? You may have asked, "Who is my real father?", but no one seems to want you to have that information. Doesn't life sometimes make you want to throw your hands up and holler? So, what are your hard questions for God? I know you have some. Do you believe that if you ask those questions, you can expect answers?

In chapter two of the book of Habakkuk, we find Habakkuk *expecting* God to answer him. This guy actually climbed up to a watchtower and stood at a guard post to wait for God's answer! It makes me wonder just how serious we are about expecting to hear from the Lord. We, too, ought to expect answers from God when we sincerely cry out to him for help. God didn't disappoint Habakkuk, but gave him an answer to his inquiries.

Realistically, God's answer may not have been what Habakkuk wanted to hear at the time, but it still was an answer, and Habakkuk accepted it. God told him to write down His answer and then wait for the thing to happen. Now, that's where a lot of us lose it! God does eventually give us the answer to our dilemma or situation, but the waiting part can be unnerving. Just remember that eventually, we will get the answers or desires we're seeking, and He will give us peace in the meantime. In fact, God says that we can wait on our desires because it will surely happen and "not be delayed." The key is to make sure that

Habakkuk's Hardships

our desires are wrapped up in an outcome that would bring Him glory, and not something that would merely bring us fame and fortune.

Affirmations are very powerful in their effects, and Habakkuk got his directly from the God of the universe! **"The vision is for a future time. It describes the end, and it will be fulfilled. If it seems slow in coming, wait patiently, for it will surely take place. It will not be delayed."** (Habakkuk 2:3). Can you imagine the power of repeating daily an affirmation that came directly from God? Now, to understand this, you must bear in mind that God is the keeper of time, and our times are in His hands. He has an appointed time for our deliverances, so whatever change we're waiting for will not take place a second too soon, nor a second too late of God's appointed time. This should give us a tremendous amount of peace because we can be secure knowing that God is sovereign and that He's still in control of our personal situations, and the problems in the world.

Affirmations are very powerful in their effects, and Habakkuk got his directly from the God of the universe! "If it seems slow in coming, wait patiently, for it will surely take place. It will not be delayed" (Habakkuk 2:3).

I imagine that Habakkuk could easily have had a different response to God, but he chose to speak of God's sovereignty and celebrated Him for it. Habakkuk came to understand that God has His own vision for our lives and circumstances, and that He wants good things to happen for us even more than we do. Besides, God often uses our toughest challenges to shape our characters and to provide the moral and divine compasses we need for our futures. When Habakkuk saw that God was aware of his predicament, he, too, got a vision because his faith was built up. It can be very soothing to know that God is intimately concerned and involved with our predicaments and is constantly working behind the scenes on our behalf. Habakkuk's response was, **"I see God moving,"**

(Habakkuk 3:3a). That's a very powerful statement to me. The thing I want you to see is that at the time Habakkuk said that, *nothing* was moving around him; but through the eyes of faith, he saw all kinds of stuff happening! We also need to see God moving because otherwise we can easily become discouraged. The affirmation, *"I see God moving,"* should be our battle cry!

What do you see? Look closely. Can you see God moving in your situation in the spirit realm? Can you see your body healed, your finances back on track, your mind in a state of peace, or your marriage mended? You first have to get a spiritual vision of the thing coming to pass before there can be any physical or tangible evidence of it. Otherwise, you'll lose hope. You have to see God moving by faith. The scriptures says **"the just shall live by faith."** (Romans 1:17; KJV). Our faith is what jump starts our hope, and confirms to us that the vision will surely come, though it has been delayed by setbacks, losses, discouragement and pain.

Look closely. Can you see God moving?

Habakkuk carried it further by saying that though the present state of Israel seemed bleak, he would still rejoice in the Lord. Whew! How much more peace would we have if we would but respond to our *between* phases the way Habakkuk did? Like Habakkuk, we need to learn to rejoice in the Lord *before* our changes happen. He said, **"Even though the fig trees have no blossoms, and there are no grapes on the vines; even though the olive crop fails, and the fields lie empty and barren; even though the flocks die in the fields, and the cattle barns are empty, yet I will rejoice in the Lord! I will be joyful in the God of my salvation!"** (Habakkuk 3:17-18). How could God not bring His wonderful promises to pass when we develop that kind of attitude?

Let's recap Habakkuk's issues and his response to how God chose to deal with him concerning them.

90

Habakkuk's Hardships

- surrounded by violence and destruction
- in the beginning, he experienced frustration because it seemed that God wasn't listening to him
- lived in the midst of a perverted justice system

Habakkuk's Response

- asked God some hard questions
- listened to God's instructions
- allowed his faith to reign supreme over his emotions
- rejoiced in the Lord and praised God in spite of the fact that things seemed to be at a standstill
- saw in the spirit realm that God was working behind the scenes to affect changes in his life

Chapter Fifteen

David's Dilemma

> *In spite of everything, God had great plans for David's future.*

David was anointed Israel's King at a young age, but he experienced a lot between that time and the time he assumed the throne. It's interesting to note that David was chosen to succeed Saul, even though he was the youngest of all of Jesse's sons and only a shepherd boy. However, God had to remind the prophet Samuel that when He wants to use someone, He looks at the integrity of one's heart and not at their brawn or outer beauty. God often uses ordinary, unassuming people to get things accomplished. Clearly, the last thing on young David's mind was becoming one of Israel's kings.

David's story begins with the Lord having to first deal with Samuel for his prolonged mourning over Saul's loss of his kingdom, as a result of his disobedience. Samuel was the prophet who had anointed Saul as Israel's first king, so it grieved him that Saul had lost his position. Let's start from that point. **"The Lord said to Samuel, 'You have mourned long enough for Saul. I have rejected him as king of Israel so fill your flask with olive oil and go to Bethlehem. Find a man named Jesse who lives there, for I have selected one of his sons to be my king.' "** (I Sam 16:1). Then, in verse 3, **"Invite Jesse to the sacrifice,**

92

David's Dilemma

and I will show you which of his sons to anoint for me." Notice, God had already decided that He was going to put David, Jesse's youngest son, in a position of tremendous power. He had great plans for David's future!

> *"The Lord will work out his plans for my life."*
> *– Psalm 138:8*

After Samuel saw all of Saul's older sons, he realized that God had another one in mind – the youngest. They sent for David while he was out in the field tending sheep. **"In the same way all seven of Jesse's sons were presented to Samuel. But Samuel said to Jesse, 'The Lord has not chosen any of these.' Then Samuel asked, 'Are these all the sons you have?' 'There is still the youngest,' Jesse replied, 'but he's out in the fields watching the sheep and goats'. 'Send for him at once,' Samuel said, 'We will not sit down to eat until he arrives.' "** Then God said to Samuel in verse 12, **"This is the one; anoint him...Samuel took the flask of olive oil he had brought and anointed David with the oil. And the Spirit of the Lord came powerfully upon David from that day on."** (I Samuel 16: 10-13).

Of particular note here is that God had a definite plan for David's future, but he was still going to have to experience many things before actually assuming the throne. In fact, God was *preparing* him for his future. Oil set people or objects apart for God's service, but I sometimes wonder if David even understood the great significance of having been anointed by the prophet Samuel, given the fact that he was so young at the time. Perhaps he didn't understand it, but that did not change the fact that God had a plan and purpose for David to fulfill. David had to endure a lot, in-between, because Saul stayed on the throne until his death, many years later.

Though David knew he was anointed to take the throne, he could not just sit around idle until his appointment. He went on with his life,

93

Between: Getting From Where You Are To Where You Want To Be

perhaps at times wondering if God had somehow meant to have Samuel anoint one of his older brothers instead. Have you ever wondered if God missed the right person, and chose you instead for some special work? When you look at your life, your frailties, your failings, and your setbacks, you might be tempted to think that you couldn't possibly be the person God would choose to use to make a positive difference in your neighborhood, your church or in the world. Just cooperate with the Holy Spirit's promptings and wait for the fulfillment of the promise or calling, even when it makes little sense to you. Do you think that by running away or feigning ignorance, you can cause God to change His mind about His plan for your life? Well, it won't; but it's up to you to work with His plan, in order to bring it to fruition. Whenever you're tempted to doubt that you are truly called to accomplish a particular task, it will help to remember this part of David's story.

> *When you look at your life, your frailties, your failings, and your setbacks, you might be tempted to think that you couldn't possibly be the person that God would choose to use to make a positive difference in your neighborhood, your church, or in the world.*

Keep in mind, that despite finding himself pressed between some difficult circumstances, David was still God's man to succeed King Saul on the throne. Also, note that David's anointing by Samuel didn't happen with any fanfare, as we're accustomed to today with big appointments like supreme court judges, presidents, and military officers. It had been a very quiet process. Yet, he had been handpicked by God himself!

So, what special task is tugging at your heartstrings today? Be assured that if God has given you a dream or a specific task to accomplish, then He will give you everything you need to get it done. Yes, you! You are indeed His person for the job. He, too, has a vision, so do you think that He would drop the ball on His own vision? God is more committed to the plan He has for your life than you probably realize.

David's Dilemma

But God's plans for our lives cannot protect us from the snares within our journeys. It's possible to be aware of the plan God has for our lives, but still question it because of the difficulties we must face on the way to the manifestation of His plan. It might be helpful to visualize ourselves right in the center of some big move or plan of God. Our difficulties in life are no hindrance to our promising futures, and we should remember that as we draw inspiration from David's life. He was always *between* things in dealing with Saul, but he chose to cooperate with God's plan to get him to his destiny, the throne of Israel. Read the account of David's life story in the first book of Samuel and see if you can draw other lessons from it that can help you with the *between* phases of your own life. His is quite an interesting story!

One of the first things David had to do after being anointed Israel's next king was to serve Saul, the reigning king. Herein lies a great lesson because it is very human to love powerful positions. But it's our *service* to others that humbles and best prepares us for our futures, though initially we may be ignorant of its benefits. David was a great harpist, and he often used that gift to drive away the evil spirits that came upon King Saul. On one particular occasion, Saul's attendants informed him that God had allowed him to be tormented by an evil spirit.

"Now the Spirit of the Lord had left Saul, and the Lord sent a tormenting spirit that filled him with depression and fear. Some of Saul's servants said to him, 'A tormenting spirit from God is troubling you. Let us find a good musician to play the harp whenever the tormenting spirit troubles you. He will play soothing music, and you will soon be well again.' 'All right,' Saul said. 'Find me someone who plays well and bring him here.' One of the servants said to Saul, 'One of Jesse's sons from Bethlehem is a talented harp player. Not only that – he is a brave warrior, a man of war, and has good judgment. He is also a fine-looking young man, and the Lord is with him.' " (I Samuel 16:14-18).

"So Saul sent messengers to Jesse to say 'Send me your son David, the shepherd.' Jesse responded by sending David to Saul, along with a young goat, a donkey loaded with bread, and a wineskin full of wine. So David went to Saul and began *serving him*. (Italics mine).

Saul loved David very much and David became his armor bearer. Then Saul sent word to Jesse asking, 'Please let David remain in my service, for I am very pleased with him.' And whenever the tormenting spirit from God troubled Saul, David would play the harp. Then Saul would feel better, and the tormenting spirit would go away." (I Samuel 16:19-23).

Notice also that immediately after David was anointed, he went right back out into the field to his old job as a caretaker of sheep! Timing is very important. Though David had been *anointed,* he hadn't yet been *appointed.* Sometimes, we have to wait on our appointments, though we might have already received the "call" to do something special. Saul had a need, and it was met through David's service. David was really *between* some things, yet he served while he waited for his time to assume the throne. And it was a long time – many years later – before that happened. In fact, during those times while David was serving Saul, Saul was not even aware that Samuel had secretly anointed David to be his successor!

Most of us are familiar with the story of David and Goliath. David was not only a shepherd boy; he was also a fierce warrior. He slew the Philistine giant with only a slingshot and a few smooth stones. However, as sweet as that victory was, it caused some problems for him. In I Samuel 18:6-8, the story continues: **"When the victorious Israelite army was returning home after David had killed the Philistine, women from all the towns of Israel came out to meet King Saul. They sang and danced for joy with tambourines and cymbals. This was their song: 'Saul has killed his thousands, and David his ten thousands!' This made Saul very angry. 'So what's this?' he said. 'They credit David with ten thousands and me with only thousands. Next they'll be making him their king!' So from that time on Saul kept a jealous eye on David."**

A jealous spirit can push an individual to do almost anything. I almost had to read this story on the edge of my seat! It's hard to believe that a king would stoop so low. Just keep reading. **"The very next day a tormenting spirit from God overwhelmed Saul, and he began to rave in his house like a madman. David was playing the harp as he did each day. But Saul had a spear in his hand, and he suddenly**

96

David's Dilemma

hurled it at David, intending to pin him to the wall. But David escaped him twice." (I Samuel 18: 10). Can you believe that? The king tried to pin David to the wall with a spear!

I find this absolutely incredible. David discovered that his fiercest battle was not in facing the Philistine giant, but in dealing with his jealous boss! Have you ever had to deal with a jealous and insecure boss? Okay, so maybe your boss didn't try to physically kill you, but did he or she try to set you up to fail and cause you to lose your job when he saw you getting the attention he or she craved?

In David's case, it surely didn't help that the women composed a praise song right there on the spot to honor him and danced to it in front of the king and everyone else. Now, David had all the *women* on his side, too! I'm not so sure that it even fazed David, but it really got King Saul's attention, and the scripture tells us that the women's song "galled him." The King was livid! He longed for that kind of attention. Listen to this again: **"From that time on, Saul kept a jealous eye on David."** (I Samuel 8:9). How sad is that?!

David discovered that his fiercest battle was not in facing the Philistine giant, but in dealing with his jealous boss!

As we continue to read David's story, we find in chapter 19, that Saul made his first of several attempts to kill David or have him killed (I Sam 19:1). The story continues. **"Saul now urged his servants and his son Jonathan to assassinate David."** Skipping down to verse11, the scriptures tell us, **"Saul sent troops to watch David's house." But David's wife gave him the heads up on Saul's plan, and devised a plan to save him and helped him escape. Yet Saul was so determined to get David that he told his men, "Bring him up to me in his bed so that I may kill him!"** (I Samuel 19:11-15). It was obvious that Saul would stop at nothing!

David went through some crazy stuff! One interesting thing worth noting is that David had more than one opportunity to take Saul's life

Between: Getting From Where You Are To Where You Want To Be

as revenge for all of the problems Saul had caused him. And he was actually in the cue to do that once, but the Spirit of God caused him to change his mind. The Bible says, **"So David crept forward and cut off a piece of the hem of Saul's robe. But then David's conscience began bothering him because he had cut Saul's robe. The Lord knows I shouldn't have done that to my lord the king," he said to his men. 'The Lord forbid that I should do this to my lord the king and attack the Lord's anointed one, for the Lord himself has chosen him. So David restrained his men and did not let them kill Saul.' "** (I Samuel 24: 4b-7). Without a doubt, David was the better man!

To make a very long story short, David spent a significant part of his life on the run from an angry, insecure, and very jealous King Saul. Throughout his life, he experienced many things, from victories and losses to both personal and moral failures. Still, God kept His promise, and David did eventually assume the throne as Israel's king following the death of Saul.

<u>David's Dilemma</u>

- anointed at a young age to succeed Saul as Israel's King, but first, he had to endure many years of hardships
- had to deal with an insecure and jealous boss
- needed to develop a strategy to get around Saul's assassination attempts on his life
- Saul was determined to keep him from assuming the throne

<u>David's Response</u>

- clung to the gracious and merciful nature of God
- became a *servant* and used his harp playing skills to soothe King Saul's often agitated soul
- chose to not retaliate by killing Saul, though he had at least two opportunities to do it

Chapter Sixteen

Joseph's Jolts

> *Perhaps, in the beginning, it's not always good to run off and tell others about our dreams. Maybe we should hold off until after we've secured those dreams in our hearts.*

Young Joseph had a couple of dreams and got so excited about them, that he shared them with his family. Well, that certainly turned out to be a bad idea. But in all fairness, Joseph had no way of knowing how his brothers would react to his dream. He got those guys all "geeked" up. (That's an expression my husband often uses, which means to upset or irritate). In Joseph's dream, he saw himself in a position of such power that his brothers and parents would one day be dependent on him for their daily sustenance. But before we get down on Joseph, let's keep in mind that he was only seventeen years old when he had this dream. Very few teenage boys are able to think through their decisions with a great level of maturity. I cannot fault Joseph for being excited about his dreams. However, his eagerness to share them got him in trouble with his family.

Joseph was a tattletale, too. He liked to tell his dad about his brothers' mischievous deeds. The scriptures reads, **".... but Joseph reported to his father some of the bad things his brothers were**

99

Between: Getting From Where You Are To Where You Want To Be

doing." (Genesis 37:2). I'm almost certain that Joseph would have never imagined that the telling of his dream to his brothers would provoke such anger and jealously, that they would want to kill him! This set into motion thirteen years of setbacks, unfair treatments, disappointments, and frustrations for Joseph.

Let's look at the backdrop of this story. Joseph was his father's favorite of all his sons. Now, that right there is enough to cause some serious sibling fights! In Genesis 37: 3-4, we find this account: **"Jacob loved Joseph more than any of his other children because Joseph had been born to him in his old age. So one day Jacob had a beautiful multi-colored robe made for Joseph. But his brothers hated Joseph because their father loved him more than the rest of them. They couldn't say a kind word to him."**

Then Joseph had a dream. What could possibly be so bad about having a dream? You'd probably agree, absolutely nothing, right? Yes, but the problem came when Joseph decided to tell his dream to his brothers, who already had some issues with him. Here's the account of the telling of Joseph's dream. **"One night Joseph had a dream, and when he told his brothers about it, they hated him more than ever. 'Listen to this dream,' he said. 'We were out in the field, tying up bundles of grain. Suddenly my bundle stood up, and your bundles all gathered around and bowed low before mine!' His brothers responded, 'So you think you will be our king, do you? Do you actually think you will reign over us?' And they hated him all the more because of his dreams and the way he talked about them."** (Genesis 37:5-8). Now, God didn't tell that boy to go off telling his dreams! I'm so glad that God stands ready to fix stuff after we've messed it all up. Perhaps, in the beginning, it's not always good to run off and tell others about our dreams. Maybe we should hold off until after we've secured the dreams in our hearts.

Now here he goes again. **"Soon Joseph had another dream, and again he told his brothers about it."** Right about here, I want to scream, *"Shut up Joseph"*! But he continued, **"'Listen, I have had another dream,' he said. 'The sun, moon, and eleven stars bowed low before me!' This time he told the dream to his father as well as**

Joseph's Jolts

to his brothers, but his father scolded him. 'What kind of dream is that?' he asked. 'Will your mother and I and your brothers actually come and bow to the ground before you?' " (Genesis 37:9-10).

Now, Joseph *really* had some problems. He was indeed *between* some things. You see, the original dream he shared with his brothers didn't come to fulfillment until Joseph was thirty years old! Initially, Joseph's brothers had plotted to kill him. Instead, because of his brother, Reuben, they decided to throw him into a waterless well out in the middle of a desert. Then they sold him into slavery. Joseph was *jolted!*

Sometime later, Joseph was thrown into prison after his boss' wife falsely accused of him of attempted rape. In Genesis 39:1-5, we read, **"When Joseph was taken to Egypt by the Ishmaelite traders, he was purchased by Potiphar, an Egyptian officer. Potiphar was captain of the guard for Pharaoh, the king of Egypt. The Lord was with Joseph, so he succeeded in everything he did as he served in the home of his Egyptian master. Potiphar noticed this and realized that the Lord was with Joseph, giving him success in everything he did. This pleased Potiphar, so he soon made Joseph his personal attendant. He put him in charge of his entire household and everything he owned."**

But just as Joseph was prospering in his job, he was suddenly set back again because of the evil intentions of an unfulfilled, lustful, and angry woman who couldn't get her way. She wanted Joseph *badly!* I like how the scriptures laid this account out so clearly. **"Joseph was a very handsome and well-built young man, and Potiphar's wife soon began to look at him lustfully. 'Come and sleep with me,' she demanded. But Joseph refused. 'Look,' he told her. 'My master trusts me with everything in his entire household. No one here has more authority than I do. He has held back nothing from me except you, because you are his wife. How could I do such a wicked thing? It would be a great sin against God.' She *kept putting pressure on Joseph day after day*, (italics mine), but he refused to sleep with her, and he kept out of her way as much as possible."** (Genesis 39: 6b-10). I'm so glad that Joseph didn't bow to the pressure! Well, as fate would have it, Potiphar's wife's evil scheme got Joseph thrown in prison anyway. *Another jolt!* Joseph must have been shaking his head by now

Between: Getting From Where You Are To Where You Want To Be

and wondering what in the world he did wrong to deserve all of this ill-treatment. However, while still in prison, the scripture says, **"The Lord was with Joseph in the prison and showed him his faithful love. And the Lord made Joseph a favorite with the prison warden."** (Genesis 39: 21).

Then Joseph met two guys in prison; a baker and a cupbearer, and he used his gift of dream interpretation to help them get out of prison. Joseph's dream interpretations were particularly favorable towards the cupbearer, who eventually got his old job back. All Joseph asked the cupbearer to do when he got out was to remember him. **"And please remember me and do me a favor when things go well for you. Mention me to Pharaoh, so he might let me out of this place. For I was kidnapped from my homeland, the land of the Hebrews, and now I'm here in prison, but I did nothing to deserve it."** (Genesis 40:14). However, after the chief cupbearer was released from prison, he totally forgot to show favor to Joseph. *The guy forgot!* The bible says, **"Pharaoh's chief cupbearer, however, forgot all about Joseph, never giving him another thought."** (Genesis 40:23). *Jolt!* He never gave Joseph another thought! How unfortunate; especially after he'd received Joseph's help.

As time went on, Joseph continued in his day-to-day living and his interpreting of dreams, and he eventually found favor with the Pharaoh. As a result, Pharaoh put Joseph in charge of all of Egypt. **"Joseph was thirty years old when he began serving in the court of Pharaoh, the king of Egypt."** (Genesis 41:46). It didn't happen overnight, but Joseph's gift of interpreting dreams truly made room for him and put him in the presence of great leaders.

What we need to take note of is how Joseph kept serving others *even* while he was in the thick of his own disappointments and setbacks. He continued to use his gift of interpreting dreams to help the cupbearer get out of prison. And he used his leadership skills, and showed great integrity towards his master Potiphar, even though Potiphar's wife lied about him and sabotaged his position. In his new leadership role in Egypt, Joseph extended forgiveness to his brothers for what they had done to him. In my readings, I couldn't find any time within that thirteen-year period where Joseph held any kind of grudge against his brothers or anyone else who had mistreated him.

Joseph's Jolts

Thirteen years is a long time to be between a dream and its fulfillment, especially when you're being battered all along the way. Isn't it interesting how Joseph dealt with his experiences between the time God gave him those dreams about his future and the actual realization of them? We can learn many valuable lessons from Joseph's life. He moved through those painful years with a resolve to handle his circumstances with extraordinary wisdom.

When Joseph finally came face to face with his brothers, he could have used his position to cause them great suffering. However, he maintained Godly integrity and chose instead to bless his brothers, and his parents. Joseph was so in tune with God that he saw the big picture and couldn't place any blame on his brothers for what they'd done to him.

Thirteen years is a long time to be between a dream and its fulfillment, especially when you're being battered all along the way.

Of course, Joseph was vindicated in the end. Here's the account of the culmination of this wonderful life story. Egypt was in the midst of a seven-year famine, but Joseph was in charge of the food distribution! What an honorable position to be put in. His brothers were in shock when Joseph revealed his identity to them because they thought that surely he'd been dead after all of those years. Remember, that their original intent had been to kill him, or at least to put him in a position to be killed, so they had no idea that Joseph had survived. Listen to this. **" 'I am Joseph!' he said to his brothers. 'Is my father still alive?' But his brothers were speechless! They were stunned to realize that Joseph was standing there in front of them. 'Please, come closer,' he said to them. So they came closer. And he said again, 'I am Joseph, your brother, whom you sold into slavery in Egypt. But don't be upset, and don't be angry with yourselves for selling me to this place. It was God who sent me here ahead of you to preserve your lives. This famine that has ravaged the land for two years will last**

103

Between: Getting From Where You Are To Where You Want To Be

five more years and there will be neither plowing nor harvesting. God has sent me ahead of you to keep you and your families alive and to preserve many survivors. So it was God who sent me here, not you. He is the one who made me an adviser to Pharaoh – the manager of his entire palace and the governor of all Egypt.' " (Genesis 45:3-8).

When Joseph told his brothers that it had been God who'd orchestrated the entire thing, it clearly showed that he had a larger view of his situation. That tells me that if we can get the larger view of our difficult times, then there will be no room to cast the ultimate blame on anyone else. Like Joseph, that should give us peace of mind. I think that perhaps the only thing that helped him to endure all those years of hardship was his assurance that God was still in control of his circumstances. Why don't you ask God to show you the big picture in your difficult situation? Like Joseph, it will help to undergird you during such times.

In my opinion, Joseph handled this situation like a champion! Talk about coming full circle! This is the stuff of which victors are made. Listen to this. **"Weeping with joy, he embraced Benjamin, and Benjamin did the same. Then Joseph kissed each of his brothers and wept over them, and after that they began talking freely with him. The news soon reached Pharaoh's palace: 'Joseph's brothers have arrived!' Pharaoh and his officials were all delighted to hear this. Pharaoh said to Joseph, Tell your brothers, 'This is what you must do: Load your pack animals, and hurry back to the land of Canaan. Then get your father and all of your families and return here to me. I will give you the very best land in Egypt, and you will eat from the best that the land produces.' "** (Genesis 45:14-17).

Look at that. Because of the way Joseph handled being between some difficult things, his entire family got blessed! Joseph remained steadfast during his thirteen-year period of innocent mistakes, setbacks, and disappointments. God elevated Joseph and granted him the highest favor; the "best of all of Egypt" for both he and his family. I would have given anything to have been there to see the look on his brothers' faces!

Joseph had a positive response to each setback. He didn't waddle in self-pity. Instead, he looked for ways to be of service to others and ways to come out of his dilemmas. What amazes me most about Joseph is that he maintained personal integrity throughout his entire ordeal and was always spiritually sensitive to God.

Pharaoh was so impressed with Joseph that he asked his officials, **"Can we find anyone else like this man, so obviously filled with the Spirit of God?"** (Genesis 41:38). I love the use of the word "obvious" because it tells us that Joseph's godly lifestyle was evident to everyone with whom he had contact. Isn't that how our lives should look to a needy world? I mean, shouldn't it be obvious, that we, too, belong to God? When we consider Joseph's track record, we see that he went from being a shepherd to a slave, from a slave to a servant, from a servant to a prisoner, and then finally from a prisoner to ruler over all of Egypt; having to answer only to the Pharaoh himself. Joseph's life story is highlighted in the book of Genesis, chapters 30 to 50.

> *Joseph had a positive response to each setback. He didn't waddle in self-pity. Instead, he looked for ways to be of service to others and ways to come out of his dilemmas.*

Joseph's Jolts

- betrayed, deserted, and left for dead by his brothers
- exposed to sexual temptation by his master's wife
- was set up to look like an attempted rapist, and punished although he did the right thing
- forgotten by the person he helped to get out of prison, and therefore had to endure a long imprisonment

Joseph's Response

- did not waddle in self-pity

Between: Getting From Where You Are To Where You Want To Be

- was always willing to help others, even throughout his long personal ordeal
- maintained the highest level of personal and Godly integrity
- didn't hold a grudge towards his brothers or anyone who had mistreated him
- showed pity on his brothers when he met them again in Egypt, seventeen long years after they threw him into a pit and sold him into slavery

Chapter Seventeen

Hannah's Hell

> *When we're wedged between some of life's difficulties, even those closest to us don't really understand our anguish. Sometimes, we just have to go straight to God with our problems.*

When I think of the prophet Samuel, I can't help but think of the time God used him to anoint Israel's first King. In fact, Samuel's name is listed in the Hall of Faith of great biblical personalities in the book of Hebrews. However, Samuel's beginning came about because of a humble God-fearing woman who was pressed between some things. Hannah had an intense desire to have a child, but she was barren. Her trial was made even worse when her husband misunderstood her anguish and thought his love for her would be enough to erase her desire to give birth to a child.

Here is Hannah's story from the beginning of the book of Samuel: **"There was a man named Elkanah who lived in Ramah in the region of Zuph in the hill country of Ephraim...Elkanah had two wives, Hannah and Peninnah. Peninnah had children, but Hannah did not. Each year, Elkanah would travel to Shiloh to worship and sacrifice to the Lord of Heaven's Armies at the Tabernacle. The priests of the Lord at that time were the two sons of Eli, Hophni and**

107

Phinehas. On the days Elkanah presented his sacrifice, he would give portions of the meat to Peninnah and each of her children. And though he loved Hannah, he would give her only one choice portion because the Lord had kept her from having children. Year after year, it was the same – Peninnah would taunt Hannah as they went to the Tabernacle. Each time, Hannah would be reduced to tears and would not even eat. 'Why are you crying, Hannah?' Elkanah would ask. 'Why aren't you eating? Why be downhearted just because you have no children? You have me – isn't that better than having ten sons?' " (I Samuel 1:1-8). After reading this, I thought, *Oh no! Did he really ask her if having him wasn't better to her than having ten sons? No,* Elkanah, *no!* I almost cannot believe he asked her that!

Now, let's look at Hannah's live-in rival. I can only imagine that having to endure Peninnah's on-going taunts must have been akin to a living hell for Hannah. Anyone who knows me well knows that one thing I have zero tolerance for is taunting. My children can tell you how many times they've heard me say that I won't allow taunting in our family because I think that we should be one another's biggest cheerleaders. I've been on both sides of this kind of thing, and either way it's a horrible thing. You see, once a person leaves their house, he or she may be exposed to all kinds of ill-treatment, so home must be a *haven.* I have absolutely no problem having a good time teasing with friends and family if it's in good taste, but teasing and taunting for the sake of belittling someone or attempting to soothe one's own insecurities is a horse of a different color.

We've all heard the news stories of school children, or even adults, reacting violently towards schoolmates or work colleagues as a result of heavy taunting that had been directed at them. Such behavior almost always leads to tragic endings. In Hannah's story, I'm not sure what Peninnah's point was, but as a woman, she should have at least been aware of the pain and embarrassment that accompanied barrenness, especially in their society. Barrenness caused deep internal pain and was considered a societal curse in that culture. Yet, the scriptures tell us that she was determined to drive sharp stakes into Hannah's heart over and over again. Hannah became a personal target for Peninnah, and

I'm certain that by the time she finished with her, Hannah's self-esteem was on the floor!

Let's look at this account again. **"And because the Lord had closed her womb, her rival kept provoking her in order to irritate her,"** (verse 1:6, NIV). Peninnah persistently aimed to irritate Hannah. Have you ever had someone continually provoke you for the express purpose of irritating you? Peninnah vexed Hannah to the point of causing her to lose her appetite! Again, verse 7 says, **"Each time, Hannah would be reduced to tears and would not even eat."** Have you ever been "reduced to tears" by a mean-spirited person? I'm beginning to get a glimpse of what Hannah's pain must have felt like. Look at how long she was between her desire of wanting to bear a son and the fulfillment of that desire. The scriptures don't tell us exactly how many years it was, but I get the impression that it must have been a very long time because it says, **"This went on year after year."** (verse 1:7a, NIV). *Ouch!*

> *Have you ever had someone in your life continually provoke you for the express purpose of irritating you?*

Now let's take a look at Hannah's husband. Poor fellow; he loved her dearly. In fact, he loved Hannah so much that he gave her a special portion of meat when he went up to the temple to sacrifice to the Lord. Peninnah and her children got their appropriate portions, but because Elkanah loved Hannah so much, he gave her *lagniappe*. "Lagniappe" is a word we use in New Orleans that means a little "something extra". The scriptures don't tell us whether or not Elkanah was aware of Peninnah's taunting of Hannah, but we do know that Peninnah was relentless in her attacks. Undoubtedly, she caused more insult to Hannah's already anguished soul.

Did you notice Elkanah's succession of questions for Hannah? I mean, he was on a roll! **"Why are you crying, Hannah? Why aren't you eating? Why be downhearted just because you have no children? You have me. Isn't that better than having ten sons?"**

(verse1:8). I am sure Hannah appreciated everything Elkanah had done for her and how much he really loved her, but he was really clueless. Let's be mindful of something important here. Hannah loved her husband in return and didn't complain to him, but she had the sense enough to know that her situation needed divine intervention. She had to call on God!

I'm reminded of an experience I had following Hurricane Katrina. My children and I were displaced and separated from my family, and I had no job and no money. I didn't know if my grandma Hilda or my brother Arnold were alive. Some weeks later, I found out that after learning her home had been destroyed, my Aunt Ora had suffered a heart attack and died. She was my father's sister. As you can imagine, I was depressed and confused; and I was hurting. That same day, one of my well-meaning friends, whom I love dearly, pulled me aside and said to me, "I don't know why your countenance is so sad". Then she said, "I thought that what we've done for you and your children would be enough." But then she dropped a bomb on me when she said, "I thought I could fix you." Wow. I was very grateful to my friend for reaching out to us. She really cared about me and my children, but I remember being stunned by her comment, and considered how sweet life would be if material things had the power to "fix" us.

My friend really cared about us. She just didn't want to see us hurting. It's the same way with the people in your life, who love and care about you. They hurt when you hurt. However, no one can "fix" us. Never let anyone think that they can *fix* you, and never try to convince yourself that you can *fix* another person. We truly are our "brother's keeper", but all we can do is offer friendship and spiritual, emotional, and financial support when appropriate. Then we just have to sit on the sideline and let people experience their unique journeys, even through times of difficult transitions. I know that's not easy to do. Yet, it's the only way that we can allow our loved ones to get the maximum benefit from their life's challenges.

Like Elkanah, my friend had no clue about the level of anguish I was experiencing. But like Hannah, I knew I needed to pour my heart out to God. I gave myself permission to grieve and be sad, too. Never deny yourself permission to do that! Grieving is a necessary part of the healing process. You don't have to fake like you are not hurting. Hannah's husband really thought that because he loved her, gave her choice pieces of meat, and treated her so well, that it would erase her pain of not being able to have children. Poor Elkanah, like my friend, he had a good heart. But he mistakenly thought that he could "fix" her.

But wait, the story gets even more interesting. Listen to this! **"Once after a sacrificial meal at Shiloh, Hannah got up and went to pray. Eli the priest was sitting at his customary place beside the entrance of the Tabernacle. Hannah was in deep anguish, crying bitterly as she prayed to the Lord. And she made this vow: 'O Lord of Heaven's Armies, if you will look upon my sorrow and answer my prayer and give me a son, then I will give him back to you. He will be yours for his entire lifetime, and as a sign that he has been dedicated to the Lord, his hair will never be cut.' As she was praying to the Lord, Eli watched her. Seeing her lips moving but hearing no sound, he thought she had been drinking. 'Must you come here drunk?' he demanded. 'Throw away your wine!' "** (verse 1: 9-14). That's a *head shaker* to me!

It can sometimes happen that on top of the normal frustrations of being between a pressing desire and its fulfillment, we might have to endure criticism, misunderstandings, ridicule, and accusations from others. I believe it's in anyone's best interest to learn the art of encouraging themselves because they won't always get it from others. Now, even the priest misunderstood Hannah! He thought she was drunk in church when all she was doing was asking God to remove her affliction. Simply because he couldn't hear her words, he made the assumption that she must have been high on liquor! What he didn't realize was that it was not *for* him to hear Hannah's prayer. She wasn't even talking to him. She was talking to God. This guy cracks me up!

I believe it's in anyone's best interest to learn the art of encouraging themselves because they won't always get it from others.

Between: Getting From Where You Are To Where You Want To Be

Now look at Hannah's sweet and very appropriate response in verses 15 to 16: **"'Oh no sir!', she replied. 'I haven't been drinking wine or anything stronger. But I am very discouraged, and I was pouring out my heart to the Lord. Don't think I am a wicked woman! For I have been praying out of great anguish and sorrow.'"** Hannah was a good one. I would not have even tried to explain my situation to Eli. I would have just left him to his own ridiculous thoughts.

Now you see why I have to keep studying how people in the Bible dealt with being pressed between trying circumstances. I could really use the wisdom and insight! I've got a lot to learn because I haven't always handled my stuff in ways that pleased God, though that would have been most beneficial to me. As a matter of fact, I've probably prolonged some of my suffering on occasion, simply because I didn't have the right attitude about what I was experiencing in my life. I hope that you, too, are learning lessons from Hannah.

Hannah showed Eli the utmost respect; after all, he was the temple priest. In response, Eli blessed her and pronounced God's favor upon her. Notice how God blessed Hannah. Her appetite returned, and her depression was lifted! The bible says **"… Then she went back and began to eat again, and she was no longer sad"**, (verse 1:18). God is constantly taking note of how we deal with life's challenges. You've probably heard it said many times before that it's not what happens to us but *how* we deal with what happens to us that matters. I concur. Finally, we come to the manifestation of Hannah's dream in verse 20: **"When Elkanah slept with Hannah, the Lord remembered her plea, and in *due time*, (*italics mine*), she gave birth to a son. She named him Samuel, for she said, 'I asked the Lord for him.'"** Notice that the Lord remembered how Hannah had handled her trial. Keep in mind that God keeps very accurate records. He remembers everything! You must believe that God has a "due time" concerning your situation as well.

I'm so inspired by Hannah and how she handled living between her intense desire for motherhood and its end result. She could have easily become bitter and even retaliatory towards Peninnah, but she chose not to. She could have been emotionally explosive towards her husband for not rebuking Peninnah. *And* she could have turned inward and shut down; or just retired from life altogether, but she chose not to.

112

Hannah's Hell

Have you ever become emotionally volatile in the face of extreme frustration? Don't condemn yourself if you have. It happens. Hannah responded by taking all of her hurts, frustrations, low self-esteem, and discouragement to God in prayer. She knew her only hope would come from believing in a God that was big enough and bad enough to take on her deepest longing, her husband's lack of true understanding, and her rival's mean and persistent taunting. Like Hannah, we should take our deepest longings to God in prayer, and go away confident that He will answer us too.

Hannah's Hardships

- became the personal target of Peninnah's ill-treatment and taunting
- was accused by the priest that she had come to the temple in a drunken stupor!
- experienced discouragement, great anguish, and deep sorrow while she waited for the fulfillment of her deepest desire

Hannah's Response

- was honest with God about her feelings concerning her barrenness
- didn't retaliate towards Peninnah
- showed no anger towards her husband
- allowed God to defend her cause
- *expected* God to look upon her
- sowed in tears (but reaped in joy!)

Chapter Eighteen

Ruth's Redemption

> *When we're positioned right, we put all of heaven on notice that we are ready to be blessed, though consciously our only concern at the moment is living our daily lives – yes, even when we feel like we're stuck between some things.*

Ruth was also between some things. She was between loss and redemption, financial deprivation and prosperity, and widowhood and remarriage. Still, she chose an admirable way of dealing with all of it. Let's explore Ruth's life story. **"In the days when the judges ruled in Israel, a severe famine came upon the land. So a man from Bethlehem in Judah left his home and went to live in the country of Moab, taking his wife and two sons with him. The man's name was Elimelech, and his wife was Naomi. Their two sons were Mahlon and Kilion. They were Ephrathites from Bethlehem in the land of Judah. And when they reached Moab, they settled there."** (Ruth 1:1-2). **"Then Elimelech died, and Naomi was left with her two sons. The two sons married Moabite women. One married a woman named Orpah, and the other a woman named Ruth. But about ten years later, both Mahlon and Kilion died. This left Naomi alone, without her two sons or her husband."** (Ruth 1:1-3).

114

Ruth's Redemption

From the previous verses, we see the chain of events that led to Ruth marrying a man from Judah. Her husband's parents had left Judah because there had been a famine there. They relocated to Moab where Mahlon and Kilion met and married Ruth and Orpah. However, nearly ten-years later, both Ruth, and Orpah became widows also. Ruth lost her father-in-law, brother-in-law, and husband. Her only remaining close relatives were her mother-in-law and sister-in-law. These circumstances provided her the perfect opportunity to remain in her homeland (Moab), and get reacquainted with her own people. But she chose instead to go to Judah with Naomi. Ruth knew full well that Naomi was grieving, too, and that she had no more sons available to take Ruth as a wife, as their custom allowed. Yet she felt a strong sense of loyalty towards the elder woman.

The three women had set out for Judah when Naomi implored both Ruth and Orpah to return to their homeland where they would have the greatest chances of meeting potential suitors and being married again. Notice how considerate Naomi was of the younger women. **"But on the way, Naomi said to her two daughters-in-law, 'Go back to your mothers' homes. And may the Lord reward you for your kindness to your husbands and to me. May the Lord bless you with the security of another marriage.' "** (Ruth 1:8-9). I believe it takes a special person to see beyond their needs to acknowledge the needs of others; and Naomi was obviously that kind of person.

Now look at Ruth. Even though she was aware that broken-hearted Naomi had nothing to give her, she decided to stay with her mother-in-law anyway. Orpah, on the other hand, decided to stay in Moab, which was certainly her God-given right. She was just being practical, and certainly Naomi's suggestion made a lot of sense. Naomi understood practical decisions. After all, ten years earlier, her husband made the decision to leave Judah because they had no food! What could be more practical than that? Perhaps Ruth followed a different path because she had a closer relationship with Naomi. In their society, widows were looked down upon and basically ignored, not to mention that they usually had very few resources after the death of their husbands. Ruth understood how differently their society would view her in light of her widowhood; still, she

Between: Getting From Where You Are To Where You Want To Be

remained loyal to Naomi instead of being preoccupied with getting another husband.

> *Orpah decided to stay in Moab, which was certainly her God-given right. She was just being practical, and certainly Naomi's suggestion made a whole lot of sense.*

Ruth's memorable reply to Naomi was, **"Don't ask me to leave you and turn back. Wherever you go, I will go: wherever you live, I will live. Your people will be my people, and your God will be my God. Wherever you die, I will die, and there I will be buried. May the Lord punish me severely if I allow anything but death to separate us!"** (Ruth 1:16-19). I doubt that Ruth had any idea that her decision to stay with Naomi would lead her to her divine purpose and bring even more blessings to her. It seems to me that at the time Ruth was more concerned about *giving* rather than *receiving*. She may have not even been aware of the eternal principle of giving – that if you give, it will be given back to you thirty, fifty, and one hundred fold. Ruth only wanted to serve Naomi's God, the God of Israel. She wanted to associate with a people that were called out to be God's chosen.

Honestly guys, I would have struggled with this one. I'm not sure, but, I think I may have done what Orpah did. She stayed home (in Moab), with her people. It's not always easy to leave what's familiar to go to a place and a culture where things are completely different. Besides, she wanted another husband! I can't say that I blame her. For Naomi, there was a purpose in returning to Judah, since the famine had ended. Besides, she had no other reason to stay in Moab. For Ruth, it was more of a calling. Ruth's commitment to Naomi caused her to be in the right place, at the right time, so that she could meet the right man, who would do the right thing with her. Ruth could have allowed herself to become bitter because of her losses, but instead she stayed humbled and determined to do what she deemed the right thing for her

116

Ruth's Redemption

life. I'm encouraged by the "rightness" of it all. And I'm very impressed by Ruth's focus.

Ruth was from the Moabite culture, a heathen culture that couldn't have cared less about worshipping the true God. The Lord honored Ruth's courage and showed her favor through a man named Boaz, who would eventually become her new husband. It's interesting to note that Boaz was actually related to Naomi's deceased husband, but because Ruth was associated with Naomi, she indirectly became associated with Boaz.

There's a lot to be said about noble intentions, and Ruth's gracious spirit ushered in a type of redemption for her. One typical morning Ruth got up to go to get food for herself and for Naomi. She was new to the community, so she knew that, at best, she might be able to go to the field to gather leftovers from anyone who was willing to show her goodwill. In Ruth 2:2, we read, **"One day Ruth the Moabite said to Naomi, 'Let me go out into the harvest fields to pick up the stalks of grain left behind by anyone who is kind enough to let me do it.' Naomi replied, 'All right, my daughter, go ahead.' So Ruth went out to gather grain behind the harvesters. And as it happened, she found herself working in a field that belonged to Boaz, the relative of her father-in-law, Elimelech."**

While Ruth was working, Boaz, the owner of the field, noticed her, (the new girl), and inquired about her: **"Then Boaz asked his foreman, 'Who is that young woman over there? Who does she belong to'?"** (verse 2:5). Did Ruth get his attention or what!? Eventually, Boaz approached her and said to her, **"But I also know about everything you have done for your mother-in-law since the death of your husband. I have heard how you left your father and mother and your own land to live here among complete strangers. May the Lord, the God of Israel, under whose wings you have come to take refuge, reward you fully for what you have done."** (verses 2:11-12).

Follow along with me to understand the next pivotal moment in Ruth's journey! In verses 3:1- 6, the story continues. **"One day Naomi said to Ruth, "My daughter, its' time that I found a permanent home for you, so that you will be provided for. Boaz is a close relative of ours and he's been very kind by letting you gather grain**

117

Between: Getting From Where You Are To Where You Want To Be

with his young women. Tonight he will be winnowing barley at the threshing floor. *Now do as I tell you,* (Italics mine) – take a bath and put on perfume and dress in your nicest clothes. Then go to the threshing floor, but don't let Boaz see you until he has finished eating and drinking. Be sure to notice where he lies down; then go and uncover his feet and lie down there. He will tell you what to do."

"I will do everything you say," Ruth replied. So she went down to the threshing floor that night and followed the instruction of her mother-in-law."

My point here is to show you that while Ruth was in the thick of tough *between* situations she was obedient to Naomi's wise advice. Additionally, she remained dedicated to high moral standards and soaring integrity. As a result, the events of Ruth's life were ordered in such a way that a wealthy businessman married her, thereby making provisions for both Ruth *and* Naomi. To Ruth's credit and benefit, she followed the counsel of the elder woman and remained teachable. Go Ruth!

> *Ruth could have allowed herself to become bitter because of her losses, but instead she stayed humbled and determined to do what she deemed the right thing for her life.*

We'll never know, but maybe Ruth *did* second guess herself during this *between* phase of her life. It's possible that she may have questioned herself. *"Should I have stayed in Moab? I bet Orpah probably has another man by now. I can really imagine myself with a fine Moabite man."* Well, if she *did* think twice, that voice was silenced as she held on to her commitment to be loyal to the widowed and aging Naomi. In the end, Ruth was at peace with her decision to follow Naomi back to Judah. This tells me that when we walk in the will of God, we too, can have peace about the decisions we make.

Ruth's Redemption

Let me encourage you to read the entire book of Ruth to glean from this incredible story. Her experience is a wonderful precursor to the ultimate redemption story.

Ruth's Rocky Road

o faced with sudden widowhood due to the death of her husband
o lost her father-in-law and brother-in-law as well
o took on the responsibility of caring for her aging mother-in-law
o was on the verge of suffering financial lack and public scorn

Ruth's Response

- maintained loyalty to her widowed and elderly mother-in-law, and to Israel's God
- determined to not allow bitterness to take root in her heart
- showed tremendous courage (did not succumb to any fear she may have felt)
- was obedient to Naomi's counsel to groom herself and go to the threshing floor where Boaz would be after work (this caused Ruth to be in the royal line of Jesus because she became the great-grandmother of David!)
- displayed character traits of kindness, integrity, and faithfulness throughout her trials

Chapter Nineteen

My Reflections on the Biblical Characters

> *I got to thinking about Habakkuk's commitment to rejoice in the Lord. Suddenly, it all made sense to me, and I found myself doing and saying the same.*

Not too long ago I got to thinking really hard about these biblical life depictions. And I think it's only fitting for me to tell you how I'm most impacted by them. I wish I could tell you that I'm writing an inspirational book merely for the purpose of honing my writing skills. Truth is, as I'm reaching out to be a blessing to you, its helping me to get through my own stuff. It's just me thinking out loud on paper; and it's been both revealing and cathartic for me. Hopefully, though, you too will find something in it to help you along your way.

I remember having a gut-wrenching time with God on one particular morning; complete with intense prayer, tears, anger, frustration, and emotional pain. You see, I'm currently *squeezed* between some things, and at the present time, I'm most in touch with the way Habakkuk felt. No, our vision is not the same, but I still have a vision, and I, too, had some hard questions for God. I told God, *I have this dream. You gave it to me, and I've done everything I know to do to stir up the gift and put it to good use".* Then I asked Him, *"So God, what's up with the delay? Why is my life in constant*

120

My Reflections on the Biblical Characters

transition? Why does it seem like I'm not making progress? Why can't I get out of this ditch?" I just want the fulfillment of the dream to hurry up and tarry no more! (I can laugh at this now, but it wasn't funny then).

Habakkuk

Like Habakkuk, I've written my vision down. In fact, I've written it down so many times that I cannot begin to tell you where they all are! I've written my vision in fancy journals, on memo pads bought from drug stores, in 3-subject notebooks, and on paper towels from my kitchen. I've also written it in the margins of whatever book I was reading at the time, and even on the condensation-covered glass front door of my home! And still, I'm waiting, though the vision tarries.

I really needed a good cry that morning when I took my hard questions to God. Have you ever needed a good cry? I'm glad I offered myself no restraint that day. I mean, I let God have it, and I must have cried enough tears to refill an emptied out Mississippi River! Then I got to thinking about Habakkuk's commitment to rejoice in the Lord. Suddenly, it all made sense to me, and I found myself doing and saying the same. I picked up my Bible and read the scripture where Habakkuk acknowledges that *everything* in his life had dried up - no blossoms, no oil, no anything!

Let's review what he said. **"Even though the fig trees have no blossoms, and there are no grapes on the vines; even though the olive crop fails; and the fields lie empty and barren; even though the flocks die in the fields, and the cattle barns are empty, yet I will rejoice in the Lord! I will be joyful in the God of my salvation"** (Habakkuk 3: 17-19). I thought to myself *"that is me, right now, because my stuff seems to have dried up too".* "Okay, Denise", I thought. *"Girl, you better get yourself together and give God praise and thanks just because He is God!"* Realizing this set me free. It turned out to be a good day after all. Praise and rejoicing in the Lord have a way of putting things in the right perspective. And doing so can spare us a lot of anguish.

121

Between: Getting From Where You Are To Where You Want To Be

> *Praise and rejoicing in the Lord have a way of putting things in the right perspective. And doing so can spare us a lot of anguish.*

Ruth

I then thought about my girl, Ruth. I can relate to her issue also. No, I didn't lose a husband through death, but divorce can feel just as devastating. For me, it was like a death. I held out for ten years before marrying again because there was simply no need to rush into another relationship. I just needed to stay with God. Then, many years later, He allowed my path to cross with the man who was to become my new husband. I guess, like Ruth, I happened to be gleaning in the right place and at the right time when I met him. I was teaching an adult Vacation Bible School class the night I met him. I'm sure it was an appointed moment. We married in June of 2007.

Hannah

Hannah's story just *makes me twitch*! (I borrowed that expression from my daughter). If I had had to endure Peninnah's taunts, I think there would have been a little *rumbling* in that house! Then, I would have given her a piece of my mind, and in my own way, I would have let her know that she was barking up the *wrong* tree. And I probably would have tried to put some pressure on Elkanah to deal with her. Then again, when I think about it, had I handled things my way, I probably would still be barren! I would have surely gotten in God's way and tampered with His divine plan. Darn! I guess some things just get the best of me. Hannah is a much better woman than I am!

David

To me, David's situation is just plain crazy! I simply cannot imagine what it must have been like for him to have spent a good portion of

My Reflections on the Biblical Characters

his life on the run. He was constantly in and out of caves and running from that madman, Saul. It's interesting that he even had the support of Saul's own son, Jonathan, to help protect him from the very jealous king. Jonathan knew his father was insane, so he did everything in his power to help David. He knew that David was a man of integrity and had served his father well. Incidentally, David actually had a couple of opportunities to take Saul out, but he chose otherwise.

Had David responded differently to Saul's attacks, he would have forfeited his right to the throne and thwarted the plan of God for his future. We need to keep these things in mind. When we give in to our natural human bents when dealing with life's toughest situations, we may very well delay the bright future that God has planned for us or even abort it all together. We've got to stay in the game and get in the Spirit if we want to see the manifestation of God's will in our lives. (*That little admonition is especially for me!*)

> *When we give in to our natural human bents when dealing with life's toughest situations, we may very well delay the bright future that God has planned for us or even abort it all together.*

Joseph

Joseph's dream and his mistreatment by his jealous siblings yanked at my heart strings, too, that morning. I have a whole bunch of questions about his story. I wondered if Jacob ever realized that he unintentionally contributed to Joseph's brothers' hatred towards him. After all, Joseph was the only son for whom Jacob had a multi-colored coat made. It also didn't help that Joseph liked to snitch on his brothers. But did they really have to throw him into a pit like that? And did they have to sell him into slavery!? How could a bunch of siblings collaborate on such a level to actually rid themselves of one of their own? At least Reuben had a little mercy on Joseph and talked his brothers out of killing him.

Between: Getting From Where You Are To Where You Want To Be

Joseph was an amazing young man, and he grew up to be an awesome leader. Remember that. He prospered *anyhow.*

At the time I felt impressed to highlight the lives of these particular biblical characters I had no idea that I would be so deeply affected by them. I thought I was just doing some good writing and Bible teaching on paper. But being stuck between things can be a very exciting time because, with hope, we can look forward to the manifestation of God's plan in our lives. With hope, we're encouraged to not give up. And through hope, we're fueled to maintain a certain level of enthusiasm. I've learned to appreciate these challenging intervals in my life, and I know I will become a wiser woman because of them.

In summary, I really believe that we will claim more personal victories in our lives if we do as these people did. David cooperated and served, Ruth chose wisely and remained loyal, Hannah prayed and expected a miracle, Joseph served and forgave, and finally, Habakkuk asked hard questions and rejoiced. So, what is your take on these biblical stories? As with the other chapters, I've included some thought-provoking questions for you.

Questions to Ponder

1. Are you surprised by some of the hardships, setbacks, frustrations, or consequences to mistakes that some biblical personalities had to endure?
2. Which character most reminds you of how you've dealt (or perhaps how you're currently dealing) with a *between* phase in your life?
3. Which character is most *unlike* the way you've dealt with uncomfortable *between* periods in your life?
4. Which biblical character inspires you the most, and why?

Dare To Do This

Pick out one of the Bible characters and do exactly what he or she did to get through his or her *between* periods. See if it will make a positive difference in how you endure your crisis.

Chapter Twenty

Afterthoughts

> *There had been a tug of war between my reality and my dream, and my dream won out. That's what I want for you; for your dream to win out.*

Six years ago, I started writing a book. It was supposed to be a novel, or so I thought. But when I started writing, it just would not come! So I put away the floppy disk that bore my poor attempt. Darn. Why couldn't I just write a novel? It would have been a perfect place for me to hide. I could have gotten right into some of the characters, and no one would have known that I was talking about my own issues. That pitiful attempt at novel writing will probably haunt me forever. But that's okay. I've accepted that it just wasn't supposed to happen that way. Otherwise, I might be tempted to change my mind and make up some fictitious people whose stories could all be mine, enclosed in an eye catching book cover.

On the other hand, this book is alive; it's a living, breathing thing that is me, on paper. It wasn't supposed to turn out like this, I swear to you. In fact, it's so alive that I sometimes hear the manuscript beckoning me to come, not for any revisions, but to gain insight from its pages. I trust that I've done right by you, by God and by myself. I know that, once this life account is released into the world, I won't be able to take it back.

Between: Getting From Where You Are To Where You Want To Be

I've shared with you a part of my soul, as well as my anguish. Now you know about the kinds of things that make me cry and the kinds of things that make me want to throw my hands up and holler. I've also shared with you the hopes, joys, and great expectations that are before me. I lay bare now before you, having shared with you the culmination of the woman I've become, thus far. But I have learned that, at my age, (or at any age for that matter), you just have to release some things and trust that, in time, healing and peace will find its way to you.

I'm holding myself accountable to what I've written here. This is real life – no fluff, no jokes. I have to live this stuff. And *I am responsible for it*, I tell myself. Sometimes, though, I want to run back to the novel that never was. I often envy writers who are novelists. Are their books their hiding places? Life won't allow me that kind of escape. It's making me face some things!

Several months ago, as life's circumstances would have it, I had to turn to my own manuscript for help. I had hit a bump, a jagged edge, *and* a pothole all in the same week, and I was resigned to abandoning this book project. Progress had been so slow, and I almost convinced myself that the vision to write this book must have been some kind of emotional mirage. So where was the tar to cover up my pothole; the sanding block to smooth out my jagged edge; or the jackhammer to take away the bump in my road?

Peer reviews of my book were coming back to me at a snail's pace, and the money for publishing it was vanishing into a mountain of bills, car repairs, back taxes, mounting gas prices, escalating food costs, and the children's many needs. Consequently, my deadline for publication kept getting pushed further into the unknown future. But I couldn't do anything about it because the money just wasn't there, nor did I have a completed manuscript. Furthermore, I had grown mentally tired of the project. Then I thought about you, my readers, and decided to press on because I was committed to serving you. You didn't know this, but you encouraged me throughout this entire undertaking. Thank you!

So, for some reason unbeknown to me at the time, I picked up the binder containing a copy of my unfinished manuscript. Suddenly, I made the transition from author to everyday reader. I read and read, and as I did, I was transformed and taken to another place. *Had I really*

126

written this stuff? I don't remember now what particular chapters I read that day, but what I *do* remember is that I was grateful to the author and to God for inspiring her to write something that could help me.

After doing that, I told myself to hold on to that one string that I was still able to play and to not make comparisons of my life with the lives of my seemingly more successful friends and acquaintances. I told myself to keep pushing, keep giving, keep serving others, keep mothering my two children, and keep dreaming and growing. There had been a tug of war between my reality and my dream, and my dream won out. That's what I want for you – for your dream to win out.

I reminded myself that when the brook dries up, that's when the water would flow because God is the one who controls the water springs. Divine help will visit you when you think you won't be able to go on any further, when you want to stop believing in your own dreams, and just when you try to convince yourself that you're no longer in the race. You *are* in the race, and you will finish strong!

I would love to hear from you. I may never know what *between* phases you are going through. But what I *do* know is that if you've gotten this far in the book, you have trusted me to encourage you; and now we are forever connected. This book has been written from my heart to yours, and I'm grateful to have you in my life.

I wish you the best in all things.

A Very Special Dedication

I know that it's unconventional to put a personal dedication at the end of a book, to serve as an addendum. Nevertheless, this one is especially dear to me. You see, my sister Rosemarie, whom we affectionately call "Tang", was seemingly strong and healthy when she read the first draft of my manuscript in April 2008. In fact, she was the very first person to touch it other than myself. Initially though, I was really nervous about her opinion of my book endeavor because I've always respected her as a writer, although she never published any of her works. When I asked her to be "brutally honest" with me about her assessment, she promised me that she would be. So, I cannot tell you how relieved I was when she called me and said, *"Girl, this is a good book! I couldn't put the thing down!"* But her words both surprised and shocked me. It just meant a lot to me that *she* thought well of my first book. At first, I actually thought that she was joking with me, but I soon learned that she wasn't. Yet, for some unknown reason, I was afraid of her critiques. In fact, I feared her critiques more than I did my editor's!

Tang had been an avid reader and a very good writer for as long as I can remember. And she shared her love and gift of writing with many others, including, but not limited to, our family and her colleagues at work. Don't get me wrong, she did have some words of very constructive criticism for me. I simply took her suggestions to heart, and then wisely made the improvements. Initially, I'd wondered if she would be able to separate me; her little sister, from the other me; the author. She *was* able to, and she did. But I wasn't sure if I could separate Rose Lewis Wilson, my peer reviewer, from "Tang", my big sister. Eventually, I did.

It actually dawned on me that I had to trust that if she could separate the two of "me", then I had to do the same with the two of "her". Tang made me believe in this project more than anyone else has, and she encouraged me to go forth with my dream to publish it.

Then she took things to a whole new level by contacting different book clubs and some well known personalities to ask how I might be able to market my book through their venues. I told her, *"Tang, slow down! All I have is a rough draft of a manuscript!"* But she told me that she was just that proud of me, and really excited about my work. Then she appointed herself as my public relations person. I laughed at her; she was serious with me.

I had hoped to put a hard copy of the published project in her hands before this summer's end, but that chance won't come now. Sadly, Tang was diagnosed with pancreatic cancer in July of 2008 and lost her battle to that very aggressive disease on the morning of March 26, 2009. Her belief in this project helped to keep me devoted to it, to its completion, because whenever I sat down to work on this book, or any of my other writings, I always thought of her, and I often told her as much. It was a kind of unspoken accountability that had served me well, and that will continue to serve me, as I will always think of her whenever I write. If she were here, she would tell you that she hopes you enjoyed this finished project as much as she enjoyed reading the manuscript.

Now, all I can do is hope that she got her wish.

About the Author

Denise Lewis Christopher
Author & Inspirational Speaker

    Denise Lewis Christopher began her public Inspirational Speaking and Bible teaching outreach 30 years ago, but her love for writing and speaking started at an early age. Her giftedness continues to impact people of all ages, races, and socio-economic backgrounds through compelling, insightful and authentic messages, as she often uses the most challenging parts of her own life story as a springboard to inspire and uplift others.

    Denise is the founder of L.I.F.E.Talk Communications, her writing and speaking endeavor, which seeks to motivate others to positive action and guide them along a spiritual path that would lead them to experiencing God's highest and best for their lives. She is happily married, and is the proud mother of two teenage children. She currently resides with her family in northern Virginia.

I Would Love To Hear From You!

Whatever your journey; whatever your vision; whatever your task; let me hear from you!

I told you that we're making this journey together, but in order to do that, we have to stay in touch with one another.

You can write to me at:
Denise Lewis Christopher
L.I.F.E.Talk Communications
P.O. Box 451
Fairfax Station, VA 22039-0451

Online: www.lifetalk.biz
By email: dlewischristopher@lifetalk.biz or dlewchris@yahoo.com

Printed in the United States
153740LV00005B/100/P